In India, the politicians blame the bureaucrats who, in turn, blame the politicians and both are pilloried by intellectuals who moan in public at endless seminars that the country is run by nincompoops. Seminar over, they line up outside the offices of those very nincompoops looking for trips abroad or generous research grants to study why it rains more in Cherapunjee than it does in Vijayawada and where the blame for this slight of nature lies. Abroad, our intellectuals queue up outside the offices of Western nincompoops looking for crumbs with fancy names like sabbaticals, research programmes, training courses, etc., to study why Kashmir is burning, why India doesn't get adequate investments from abroad and why our country at 50 has pimples like an adolescent and is this due to some Western genesnobbery perpetuated on an unsuspecting thumb sucking nation.

■ ■ ■

In most civilised societies and more so in civilised democracies, the adult and intelligent response to national needs and priorities is fuelled by debate, some amount of national soul-searching and a healthy exchange of views including learning from "others" if they have something worthwhile to propose. We — leaders, policy makers, you and me — have nothing to learn because we go back thousands of years and our first lot of cities were in ruins when the developed world was still in the middle and dark ages, and we had elaborate waterways and toilets when the West was still going behind the trees. And talking of trees, we were hugging them when the West was full of bushmen. So we don't need to be lectured to. Thank you!

■ ■ ■

It's a feeling of anger, disgust, frustration and, finally, helplessness that hits people like me who have to report about what our national leaders do when they claim to speak for us in the international arena. The difference comes only in the much worse form for having to explain to an international audience all the time that this is not the real India and most Indians are not as stupid as their politicians. This of course leads everyone to ask how such caricatures make it to the highest offices in the country....

■ ■ ■

India is probably the only democracy in the world where intellectuals wear their brain on their sleeves. In other parts of the civilised world, thinkers draw attention away from themselves and light-seekers are identified for what they are. In other parts intellectuals come from all walks and all sections of societies. In India they come from circles so closed and incestuous that ultimately they become irrelevant to the country's needs.

■ ■ ■

If you haven't noted it by now, you should — the Indian intellectual has India's interest in his heart, mind, pocket and gait. That is why he is hardly in the country and, from distant spots, he "intellectualises" about where India went wrong and why he was right about India going wrong even before India knew it was going anywhere.

■ ■ ■

Davos is a big showroom where you display your country, your industry, and your services.... To this forum India sends politicians who are armed not just with their ignorance of Indian and international politics but also with a long list of complexes.... In fact, nothing is more entertaining than watching our *netas* alternate between abject servility, say, in the presence of the World Bank chief to breath-taking arrogance in their dealings with lesser white mortals.... No other country in the world views multinationals with such a mixture of dread and envy as Indian politicians do. No other country's politicians beg for money from one side of the mouth while criticising the ways of their donors with the other as our politicians do.

■ ■ ■

The joke about Indian politicians is that very few of them can speak about the country's economy, trade and society with facts, figures and confidence and most of them begin and end every sentence with the words: "As the prime minister was telling me the other day..." and expect the audience to be impressed. Fine by AICC standards, but in Davos, where there is a prime minister falling out of every nook and corner, such comments make the world feel sorry for them and Indians sorry for India.

■ ■ ■

Our *netas* may be totally debauched in private, but, in public and in Davos, invite them for a glass of beer or wine and watch them jump. They will only drink tea during the day (and a soft drink at dinner) and make a virtue out of their complex by telling a foxed president of the German Bundesbank or the head of the FBI or the CEO of an Italian multinational,

"I am a social drinker" and proceed to extol the virtues of all sorts of abstinence. The bottom line in all this is their vision of a world that the West has money but no morals, and that we in India have all the morals including the moral right to beg from those we despise.

■ ■ ■

In the Western world, governments have globalised *with*, and not at the expense *of*, their people. It has been painful, but it has been done. Where did we go wrong? Which globe will we be standing on in the next century if we are led by people who make a virtue out of their stupidity?

■ ■ ■

One fine day, Western governments got an idea. They decided to infiltrate the NGO movements in the developing countries to get a mudside view of how the poor lived, died and were arbitrarily detained in prisons by dictators. The government of India hit on a better idea. It itself became an NGO, donned a wig, a moustache and let itself loose on the world stage. The GONGO — government non-governmental organisation — was born.

■ ■ ■

You would be a fool if you think that, post-CTBT, thousands of nuclear scientists cheerfully cleaned their desks and packed their bags and prepared to go fishing for the rest of their lives. There is every indication that the opposite is happening and the CTBT, like its cousin, the NPT, is a farce.

INDIA
IS FOR SALE

Chitra Subramaniam

UBSPD
UBS Publishers' Distributors Ltd.
New Delhi • Mumbai • Bangalore • Chennai
Calcutta • Patna • Kanpur • London

UBS Publishers' Distributors Ltd.

5 Ansari Road, New Delhi-110 002
Phones : 3273601, 3266646 ☆ Cable : ALLBOOKS ☆ Fax : (91) 11-327-6593
e-mail: ubspd.del@smy.sprintrpg.ems.vsnl.net.in
Apeejay Chambers, 5 Wallace Street, Mumbai-400 001
Phones : 2046971, 2047700 ☆ Cable : UBSIPUB ☆ Fax : 2040827
10 First Main Road, Gandhi Nagar, Bangalore-560 009
Phones : 2263901, 2263902, 2253903 ☆ Cable : ALLBOOKS ☆ Fax : 2263904
6, Sivaganga Road, Nungambakkam, Chennai-600 034
Phone : 8276355 ☆ Cable : UBSIPUB ☆ Fax : 8270189
8/1-B, Chowringhee Lane, Calcutta-700 016
Phones : 2441821, 2442910, 2449473 ☆ Cable : UBSIPUBS ☆ Fax : 2450027
5 A, Rajendra Nagar, Patna-800 016
Phones : 652856, 653973, 656170 ☆ Cable : UBSPUB ☆ Fax : 656169
80, Noronha Road, Cantonment, Kanpur-208 004
Phones : 369124, 362665, 357488 ☆ Fax : 315122

© Chitra Subramaniam

First Published 1997
First Reprint 1997
Second Reprint 1997

Chitra Subramaniam asserts the moral right to be identified as the author of this work.

All rights reserved. No part of this publication may be reproduced or transmitted in any form or by any means, electronic or mechanical, including photocopying, recording, or any information storage or retrieval system, without prior permission in writing from the publisher.

Cover design and illustration : R K Laxman

Designed & Typeset at UBSPD in 12 pt. Goudy
Printed at Pauls Press, New Delhi

To
*Nitya, Nikhil and Giancarlo
and dear Regina
towards whom my debts
are manifold*

Though the situations drawn in this book are from real experiences, the names and characters portrayed are the product of the author's imagination. Any resemblance to any person, living or dead, is entirely coincidental.

Contents

1. Nobody Lets India Down Like Indians   1
2. Save Kashmir   21
3. Waiting for GoDOT   53
4. When Davos Slept...   77
5. Why Does India Buy Almonds from California?   95
6. Intellectwar Singh Paperwala   129
7. Globalisation: Is It Truly Global?   143
8. GONGOS   171
9. NTPC, XYKZ, CTBT or National Defence   189
10. Index   215

1 / Nobody Lets India Down Like Indians

If I wanted to tell you something about this book in a few words, I'd say it's a little about growing up pains and a lot about those needless pains that plague you when you refuse to grow up. It is about feeling ashamed when you should actually be feeling good and feeling good when there is real reason to be ashamed. It's about asking the Vedas to decipher your past and the World Bank to predict your future while your present falls apart in front of you. It's about behaving like an irresponsible adolescent at 50.

The book could as easily be called passing the buck, Indian style. You know, this inexplicable attitude towards ourselves and the world exterior that prevents you and me from taking responsibility for our actions, our politicians from standing up for what is good for the country, and our country from telling the world India's priorities are as important as any other country's. The result is a confusion and perversion of ideas which reads something like this — give us a line and we will make it into a whole production. Have you, for instance, understood why it is alright to have Miss Delhi, Bombay, Calcutta and India contests where girls wear swimsuits, while Miss World sets the country and India's reputation as a responsible nation on fire? What is this long whining sound about Indian values? When was the last time you saw a Hindi, Tamil or a Telugu film? Why do we moralise all the time? The thumb rule suggests that people often gripe about what they don't have...!

This moanful sound — it's coming from everywhere. Put your ear to the ground. Go on, listen to India. From New Delhi to New York to Giridih to Gummidipundi there's that low-pitched grating sound. Put your ear to the wall. India's walls. Stick your ear in where decisions that affect your life and your country's destiny are made. There's that whine which says it's all their fault. Whose? Theirs? Who is "they"?

They? Doesn't matter who it is as long as there is someone or something else to pass the blame on to. The "they" can be anything and anyone from your neighbours to the World Bank to your boss's wife to the United States of America to Saturn and to that damn cat which crossed your path as you set out for an examination, ensuring with that one careless act that you would fail. All that effort trampled by a cat. What a karma!

Destiny oh! that wonderful multipurpose word that we use and abuse at will. Destiny, which drives some people out of caves to conquer new heights and pushes others back into pigeon-holes of suspicion and despair. Ever thought of taking destiny — whatever is possible — into your own hands and moulding the visible aspects of it with your experiences, answers and questions? Yes, yes, that's called growing up, but I told you this book was also about growing up pains. Yours, mine and our country's.

Hey, wait a minute. If I grow up, I don't get to gripe, isn't it? That's right. How long are we going to gripe? India is fifty. How many more years are we going to spend blaming the imperialists, external forces and Pakistan? Indeed, the world is an unequal place. That's why we sent our troops into Sri Lanka and called them peace-keepers. If we had the power, we'd be imperialists too. If any nation had power it would be an imperialist. Growing up and grasping that it is never easy. It means assuming the warts in your national character as human. It means taking responsibility for your good actions and learning from the bad ones. It also means going ahead in life and in the world.

But we have no warts, you see. And if we do, it's all "their" fault. Our politicians and leaders are not responsible for their actions because it is our destiny to be looted and cheated, and be lectured to about values and morals between two looting sessions, that is to say, between two general elections. We, as a nation, are not responsible for anything that is happening to us because we were colonised and brutalised and, while that might be our destiny, we will do nothing to alter it because then we will have nothing to whine about. Tell our leaders that for most Indians colonisation and brutalisation continue and you will be told that nothing can be compared to what the British did to beautiful India.

Hello? Hello, hello? Are you with me?

Champions at this blame-game are our elected representatives, the Gandhi-cap or *veshti**-clad keepers of

---

* A long stretch of cloth used for covering the lower portion of the body (by draping it around).

the nation's conscience who do not spare any occasion to blame "them" — electoral arithmetic, caste considerations, "what can I do if no one in the cabinet listens to me", etc., etc. — for their unenlightened decisions. When in a village they blame New Delhi for the village's failure to modernise, and when in New Delhi they blame the villages for the country's failure to globalise. You see, there's always an external circle to pass the buck on to, and when all else fails, there's that faceless, timeless, and ever-present destiny to blame. Karma, if you are scripture-friendly.

Abroad, we blame foreign forces for the bloodshed in Kashmir. The same external forces ("they"), we are told, are responsible for keeping India down in international trade; it is because of "them" that our telephones don't work and, had "they" not been there, our environment would have been as pristine as in the epics. Had "they" not imposed the bikini and the beauty contest on us, we would have no dowry deaths, the modesty of Indian women would not have been outraged; there would be water in our taps, electricity in our homes and food on everyone's plate. And a song on India's lips. Doesn't make sense, does it? And that's why it's called the long whining sound. Add to this pre- and post-colonial colour and other complexes and you begin to get the picture.

In India, our leaders blame New Delhi, international lending institutions, the constellations, including the newly discovered comet Hyakutake — all external forces — for the ills that have fallen on Chakradharpur, Nidadavole and Pipli. Our elected representatives also blame the bureaucrats who, in turn, blame the politicians and both are pilloried by intellectuals who moan in public at endless seminars that the country is run by nincompoops. Seminar over, they line up outside the offices of those very nincompoops looking for trips abroad or generous research grants to study why it rains more in Chirapunjee than it does in Vijayawada and where the blame for this slight of nature lies. Abroad, our intellectuals queue up outside the offices of Western nincompoops looking for crumbs with fancy names like sabbaticals, research programmes, training courses, etc., to study why Kashmir is burning, why India doesn't get adequate investments from abroad and why our country at 50 has pimples like an adolescent and is this due to some Western gene robbery perpetuated on an unsuspecting thumb-sucking nation? It's all "their" fault. If it's not the cat, it's the World Bank. If it's not the bank, it's karma or the neighbour's jealous wife who carries tales about you to the local ladies' club. There's always someone else to blame. Since it's never our fault, it can never be India's fault and all those who point fingers at this industrialising country should never lose track of the fact that we were colonised for 200 years and all our wealth was transported to fuel the West's industrial revolution which is what globalisation is all about. Anybody who says it's time to take stock and move ahead is an anti-national, a Western stooge. In this destiny and karma-ridden view of the world, blame comes easy. Responsibility doesn't.

In most civilised societies and, more so, in civilised democracies, the adult and intelligent response to national needs and priorities is fuelled by debate, some amount of national soul searching and a healthy exchange of views including learning from "others" if they have something worthwhile to propose. We — leaders, policy makers, you and me — have nothing to learn because we go back thousands of years and our first lot of cities were in ruins when the developed world was still in the middle and dark ages, and we had elaborate waterways and toilets when the West was still going behind the trees. And talking of trees, we were hugging them when the West was full of bushmen. So we don't need to be lectured to. Thank you!

You in India have a ringside view of how our politicians run the country and most of you have probably taken part in at least one discussion with friends, family or colleagues about how much better things could be done and how it hurts you to see India ranked not just with the poorest but also with the most corrupt in the world. Things make you angry, sometimes sad, but most often, the feeling that grips you is probably one of frustration followed by that of helplessness and you find that even if you don't want to pass the blame on to any constellation, that celestial body becomes at once a crutch and a beacon of hope to stay alive.

Why do people generally get angry? In most cases, it's because something they see, hear or have to cope with is incorrect, unjust and false. You try to change the situation and, when you can't, you give up in disgust. Where you give up is linked directly to where you come from and where you want yourself and your country to go. Frustrations in individuals, societies and nations deepen when the gap between what is possible and what is available is so vast that you have to pinch yourself to find out if you are sleeping or waking. When your leaders tell you they are working to safeguard your interests and you look out of the window and find prices rising at a pace that your salary cannot cope with, you wonder if they are talking about the same "interests" as yours. Destiny, karma and the neighbour's cat help a little, but if questions remain, it's because the painful process of growing up has started.

It's that same feeling of anger, disgust, frustration and, finally, helplessness that hits people like me who have to report about what our national leaders do when they claim to speak for us in the international arena. The difference comes only in the much worse form of having to explain to an international audience all the time that this is not the real India and that most Indians are not as stupid as their politicians. This of course leads everyone to ask how such caricatures make it to the highest offices in the country and then you find that you distance yourself from that spin on the sin by placing the blame on the cow belt (see, the "them" again!). The gap between what is possible and what is available is great. The frustration, anger and the pinch in the heart deepen when the possible becomes more real than what you are prepared to go along with.

The first stories then are easy and they are angry. They poke fun at our leaders who are such ready material that you can whip up a 1000-word story in half-an-hour and with half your brain fast asleep. Then comes disgust. After the 73rd report on how we made fools of ourselves here, there and everywhere, you take it for granted that our national representatives are going to fall on their faces. The good news is that you are rarely disappointed. The bad news is that when you are not disappointed, there's a lump in your throat. When you meet that rare bird who can stand up and speak for India, this large country with its beggars and free press, poverty and high tech, skilled workforce and illiterate masses, without moralising and complaining, you take a few quick breaths before the next load of politicians travel to Geneva to stifle you. It's those brief gasps of air that sustain hope before you are hit by a reality you don't recognise, much less understand. In fact, if every Indian decision maker was a confirmed fool there would be no place for a book like this.

What does it mean to be an Indian? I don't know and, for that matter, is it anything different for others? I mean what does it mean to be a Chinese, German or an American?

Several years ago a Swiss journalist asked me to explain India to her. Easy, I said. I could not have been more wrong. Explaining India to an outsider is a veritable nightmare. It's Europe times four, not just in terms of people, but also political parties and problems. The difference between North and South India is as much, if not more, than that between Sweden and Portugal, two tips of Europe. Which is the language we speak and which gods do we run to when in trouble? Go past the stereotypes — poverty, caste system, City of Joy, Silicon Valley of Bangalore and emerging economy, etc. — and you find that whatever you say about one part of India can be questioned by 10 other people in another part in such a basic way that you start wondering whether you understand anything after all. One can say that India is a poor country with a per capita income of $260, but 1 per cent of the country or 9.2 million people or one-and-a-half times Switzerland and Sweden are very rich, 200 million others, or Germany, France and the UK put together, are rich and another 300 million are just about making it rich. By this time your audience is as confused and lost as you are, but you continue. There are some 400 million Indians who are poor and at least 200 million among them can be counted among the world's poorest. Half the country can read, the other half cannot, and while a minuscule percentage consumes Kellog's, L'oreal and Benetton, millions of Indians do not have drinking water, electricity and access to basic health facilities. Is India a developed country because it has its own satellites, nuclear technology and a concentration of brains that makes the world envious of us or is it a poor country because the bottom 200 million rung of its people are as poor as in Zaire, 600,000 villages do not have electricity and the country does not have a telephone network worth the name? India is a country of "buts" where there is but that other side to every picture you hold up. The poor must think that you and I are not the real Indians and we think the same about them and some of us spend entire lifetimes running around this question which then becomes an excuse for inaction. Wouldn't we be doing ourselves and the nation a great service if we stopped asking these epic-like questions without answers and make the best of our reality which is as difficult as it is challenging and make tremendous demands, not just on our intellect and purse but also on our spirit? In a situation like ours questions about what is right and what is wrong are best answered with the final question about what is just. Our politicians, tied to electoral arithmetic and algorithms, do not have the courage to ask that vital question in the country for fear of losing the elections. They prefer to impose the impossible on us by ignoring the country's potential and its people's capabilities. India is a land of impossible possibilities and if we can get past the "who are we, what are we, who are they to tell us who we are" sound, the sky is the limit. Tell me I am dreaming, but since when is that forbidden?

Introduce into this challenging, dynamic and, often cruel, reality a typical Indian politician, let's say from Bihar or Uttar Pradesh — the powerhouses of the Indian electoral system — for whom anybody south of the Vindhyas is a Madrasi. Introduce the same person into an international setting that is as confused about India as India is about itself and that might explain the "why" of this book. This book attempts, through narration of events gathered and observed on a first-hand basis by a working journalist over several years, to make the point that if India finds itself with a nincompoop-ridden political class which, in turn, cannot shepherd a clear, national priority-driven negotiating agenda in international negotiations — which, by the way, will impinge increasingly on national policy objectives — a large part of the blame lies with us, not "them". Whether it be at the United Nations, GATT-WTO, meetings of multilateral donor organisations or just an international gathering of business and political leaders, nobody lets India down like Indians. And there is a method to this madness. The low whining sound is a way of life, a political compulsion, a national pastime. Anybody who deprives us of that right is a foreign agent.

I realise that you may accuse me of suggesting some kind of a return to the past — like a trip in search of what we were as a nation. I could also be accused of suggesting that India should allow the globe to turn without being on it, and that the country be deprived of the fruits of technological progress and intellectual processes. Let me just say here that if that is your position, then you are actually backing the basic claim that there is only one way to develop and that way has been shown by post-war Western society. Indeed, India has to live in today's world, but that cannot be at the expense of its own reality, and it is my deep conviction that real progress and development can be achieved only when the poorest in my country look to the future with hope and not with despair. It is also my belief that we do not need international lending institutions and development theorists from fancy universities to tell us where we went wrong, why we did so and how we should get out of the mess we have programmed ourselves into by paying large amounts of foreign exchange from our scarce reserves for advice we don't really require.

Our leaders tell us they want to globalise. In fact, few of them can make any public statement any more without slipping that word in. Okay. But, before anything else, should we not stop and ask ourselves how many globes there are within the country, which globe we want to be on and what price all Indians including the beggars on the streets will pay when we get into the big league, if at all we do?

If globalisation is not about removing poverty, then what is it all about? And if our leaders are not concerned about poverty and structures that sustain it, then what kind of people are we being led by? Ask any Indian finance or commerce minister what we should do with our levels of poverty and the answer often is that he has just spoken to his friend at Harvard, Stanford or Oxford who is sending him a new paper on what to do with the starving population outside Bodh Gaya. I do not believe that any theory, however sound, can explain reality and certainly not a reality as complex as ours. What our leaders now call "development" has poverty alleviation more as a slogan than as a reality that affects half of India in one form or another. It is my belief that poverty is basically a political issue and has to do as much with who controls and distributes power in society as it does with increase in foodgrains and the efficient use of water. Has it never occurred to you why, after 50 years of independence, there has not been any real transfer of power from the rich to the poor in such a way as to develop new ideologies, institutions and attitudes that would give us an identity of our own? Why is it that the relationship between our elected representatives and the people is comparable in its complexity to the exchanges between the leader and the led instead of being something more democratic? Could the reason be our own confusion about power and our relationship to it? Could it be a colonial hangover? Could citing the colonial hangover then become an excuse for inaction? Why is it that the poor in India are not seen as partners in progress rather than as an election slogan to be flogged once every five years within the country, and once every year abroad when our leaders set out on their annual begging mission to the world's lending institutions? Why is it that every time our leaders talk of honesty they need to say "I am a follower of Mahatma Gandhi", as if that were a certificate in itself? Have you ever read or come across any writings or speeches by Mahatma Gandhi where he says he is honest, not corrupt and that his heart bleeds for India? What is the real test of character — actions or words? You tell me. When the prime minister of India wails in public that nobody wants to invest in India and then adds in the same breath that 80 per cent of plan resources do not reach the people they were intended for, who is to blame? Would you, honestly, bet any money on the Indian Government?

Do you expect anyone in political India to ask these questions? Of course not, because asking them would mean wanting to grow up. And growing up also means taking independent decisions, making mistakes and, above all, learning from them. Unfortunately, we seem to be caught in a perpetual state of adolescence. We rebel a little, but eventually come home to a warm meal because we do not want to break the existing power structure and destroy the hand that feeds us. We apportion large portions of blame all around, so that everybody gets a bad conscience and we can go back to sucking our thumb. It is as if there is a national conspiracy to remain an adolescent for the rest of our lives. Gawky at 50 is odd, isn't it? Growing up means bidding goodbye to that long, low pitched sound — will we ever give it up?

Growing up is also about taking intelligent risks without losing sight of the bigger picture and if you, who is reading this book and me, who is foisting it on you, don't take those little risks, do you expect your domestic help and the vegetable vendor to do so? Is it so risky to ask who decides, for whom and with what effect?

What do you and I stand to lose if we ask those basic questions? It is my belief that the bigger picture I allude to in India will be dominated by the poor, who, 50 years after independence, must surely be wondering what freedom and independence are all about because these are words unknown to them.

Related directly to this perpetual state of adolescence is, naturally, our attitude to power which, above all, strikes me as a deal-making one. If someone more powerful than we or someone from whom we stand to gain something is corrupt, the standard response is: "Who is not corrupt?" However, if someone less powerful than we or someone from whom we have nothing to get steals, we use a very different language. For example, if our domestic help steals a little, how many of us say "who is not corrupt" to overlook that failing? Responsible adults concentrate on doing a good job instead of figuring out how to strike the best deal. It has always struck me as rather odd that we even make deals with our gods. You know, instead of saying "dear god, give me the strength to concentrate on this job and do my best", we say "dear god, I know what you are thinking but if you give me this job I will give you 108 *vadais*". A variation of that is "dear god if my husband gets this promotion I will fast every Tuesday for the rest of my life except when we have an official dinner in which case I will make up on Wednesday". The global spin on that is "dear god, if you swing that contract in my favour, I promise to donate 10 per cent of what I make to build a leprosy clinic which will be inaugurated by the prime minister. Or if you prefer, I will organise an eye camp with the district Rotary Club". I make a pact with god (*vadais*, golden crowns, etc.), I make a pact with the politician. I have to survive. This is my destiny. The politician makes a pact with the poor because he needs them all the time — at home for votes and abroad for money. And the poor — where do they turn to make a pact? Deals are struck because people do not have the stomach and the courage to try honestly and fail and succeed honestly. And a people that thinks that god needs 108-speed *vadais* also knows what the electrician, telephone exchange-*wala*, municipal councillor, the local policeman, etc., need as speed-money so that you can live in peace. They also know what our politicians need to stay in power. They blame destiny for it and then we all switch off the lights and go to sleep.

The funny thing is that we carry our Vedic and World Bank-driven baggage abroad when we sit in front of other nations and talk about India, its needs and its aspirations. This baggage is also placed squarely between us and our white foreign interlocutors to whom we look up in despair and look down with suspicion, depending on the occasion. White foreigners confuse us the most.

Surely you've noticed this — the "foreigner" whom we fawn upon and curse is the white, rich giver. Black foreigners don't exist unless they happen to be rich enough to hide their colour behind a big bank account. The Japanese we love because they give us a lot of money, and the Chinese we dislike because they have the bomb and a permanent seat in the United Nations Security Council. However, of immediate interest to our deal-making tendency are the white foreigners who dominate the world's power structures. Since we can cope with power only by bribing it, we are stuck. Generally, when our politicians are stuck they swing into the moralising mode. Since every white is a past, present or future coloniser, we let it all hang out. Psst! Why do we moralise so much?

It's hard to shake off the feeling that we often tend to judge people by morals and standards that we apply. A thief, for instance, thinks that everybody around him is a thief. A corrupt person tries to corrupt everything that touches him. Why am I telling you all this? Because it bugs me, the way we demean ourselves instead of standing up for the nation as responsible adults.

So, is the white man not corrupt? Indeed, he is like the rest of us. Is he all good? Yes, like the rest of us. What do you mean? Simply that white, pink, green, yellow and brown men and women, wherever they come from, whichever way they are heading, are like you and me — normal human beings with normal anxieties, fears and aspirations. If some nations have got ahead it's because some people have done very normal things like growing up into responsible adults which, in turn, has put responsible people in positions of power including political power. And they have done this without peeping too far back into history or too far ahead into those parts of the globe that mean nothing to them. There have been crooks among them, but we are doing alright in that sector of human activity.

How much easier life would be if we just let go a bit, stopped judging and dealing, put on our thinking caps, rolled up our sleeves and got on with the job of nation, community and character building, guided by just causes and honest choices dictated neither by the World Bank nor the Vedas (which most of us, in any case, have not read) but the reality in front?

India Is for Sale is a lot about us, our reality and a view of that reality from other realities in time, space and context.

These are accounts of how our visionless, self-respectless politicians speak for you and me in international fora making caricatures out of our national aspirations and dreams. These stories are a lot about our attitudes to power, which, in many ways, is a parable and a parody of our attitudes to life. The characters are fictional but the situations are drawn from real experiences of just another Indian straddling two cultures which hold up mirrors to each other.

What do we see when we look into our own mirrors? How long do we have to wait for a proper dialogue with ourselves and among ourselves to try and find out where we are going and why? There's a good chance that we won't find answers to all these questions unless we assume responsibility as a people and a nation.

2 / Save Kashmir

*T*he focal point for the activities of the United Nations in the field of human rights is located in Geneva at the UN Centre for Human Rights. The centre advises governments and provides technical services, where necessary, on human rights matters.

Article 1 of the UN Charter defines, as a major purpose of the UN, the achievement of international cooperation "in promoting and encouraging respect for human rights and fundamental freedoms for all without distinction as to race, sex, language or religion". The Universal Declaration of Human Rights, adopted by the UN General Assembly on 1 December 1948, is the common standard for measuring various countries' human rights records.

The UN Commission on Human Rights (UNHRC) was created in 1946 as a function of the UN Economic and Social Council (ECOSOC). One of UNHRC's first achievements was the preparation of the Universal Declaration which proclaims for men and women everywhere the right to life, liberty and security of person, freedom of expression, freedom from arbitrary arrest and detention, and freedom to fair trial, to name a few.

The 53-nation UNHRC meets for six weeks each year in Geneva. Using the Universal Declaration as a yardstick, the commission reviews observance of human rights worldwide, discusses reported violations and encourages countries to respect their populations' basic rights and freedoms. The commission appoints special rapporteurs to investigate specific countries' human rights situations as well as thematic issues such as disappeared persons, summary or arbitrary executions, arbitrary detention, religious intolerance and violations against women.

In recent years, criticism that the UNHRC has been turned into a name-calling forum has come from every part of the world. Thus, developing countries claim the commission backs a Western agenda where human rights is a new weapon, whereas the West asserts that the presence of Iraq, Iran and Cuba amongst the free of the world is a slur on the system. The West carefully avoids pointing fingers at the Asian tigers and cubs, thus fuelling criticism that business is more important than human rights. That is perhaps why China gets away on Tibet and Indonesia on East Timor. That is why Turkey can massacre the Kurds and Russia can slaughter the Chechens without so much as a slap on the wrist at the UNHRC. In 1995, the outgoing president of the commission said that the body was blatantly anti-Islamic and the only Muslim countries that never got criticised were those that had oil. Saudi Arabia has no human rights and even less respect for them, but it has a lot of oil, and a lot of space to station American troops; therefore, it does not even bother to show up at the commission's special meetings where its dismal human rights record is discussed.

This is where for the past ten years India and Pakistan have engaged in a spitting match over Kashmir. This is where India loses its sense of self-respect every year. This is where, in 1994, Pakistan asked the world to condemn India's human rights record.

"Eat, eat, can't think on an empty stomach. I'm not a communist," declared the "Loin"* of Kashmir turning to Mrs. Ainowitall, sitting next to him. "This chicken is delicious — your hands are magical," the Loin purred, licking his fingers.

Mrs. Ainowitall chortled. Washington was within grasp. A few more chickens and her husband would get that job.

"Don't worry about Kashmir — what is in the stars is in the stars. All gawds say same thing — Ram, Rahim, Krishna, Karim — all say peace and brotherhood. All is in the stars, leave everything to gawd", she tried to reassure the Loin, pointing to the ceiling and presumably the heavens beyond.

Mrs. Ainowitall, the rotund wife of Mr. Ainowitall, a senior Indian diplomat to the United Nations in Geneva, had heard all about it from her parents. Her father, a senior officer with the Indian Government (now retired), was a graduate from Government College, Lahore. Her mother too, she claimed, was a history graduate from the same college but her BA history (hons) first class degree had got left behind when the family fled to India during the partition in 1947. "I know all about Pakistan, I know, I know," Mrs. Ainowitall intoned, gently tapping the Loin's arm. "No holocaust and no Bosnia can come anywhere near what my parents saw," she said, serving the Loin a leg of chicken.

---

* Lion is "loin" to most people who went to Government College, Lahore, before and after partition. Since they are among the main actors in the Kashmir drama, the term "loin" has stuck.

The Loin (to India, but Faroukh Mashallah to his parents) nodded, but he was far from reassured. The Kashmir problem was too big, the world too small — he felt trapped. Peace and brotherhood, yes, but not land, he asserted. Kashmir was his *kismat*, his *jagir*, his profession, his script and his vote bank — daddy had given it to him. India had subsidised the rest, including stuffing ballot boxes during successive elections to declare, like in Bosnia, that a 112 per cent voter turnout wanted the Loin and his party National Confusion (NC) to run the state. New Delhi and the Loin used each other: New Delhi to say that a Muslim leader in a predominantly Muslim state in a predominantly Hindu India bore testimony to India's secular credentials and the Loin to say he was India's only hope in Kashmir. Both had a vested interest in each other. Had they wanted, both could have served as a bridge between the war-torn state and the rest of India. The two had ensured that no other leader emerged to challenge that premise. In any case, the Loin and India were trapped, like two scorpions in a bottle each waiting to sting if the other wanted out.

In fact, during the Loin's last reign in the late eighties, infiltration from Pakistan was at its height. The Loin didn't have time to note that Pakistan had slipped in arms and men by the thousands across its porous border with India. "They are very clever — the 'boys' (his term for cross-border transfer of terrorists) come during the golf season when I am away in Switzerland and London," he complained.

But that did not give Badnasib Bhutta, screaming from the other side of the fence, any right over Kashmir. "Over my dead body — she will come into Kashmir over my dead body, United Nations or no United Nations," the Loin thundered.

Earlier that morning the Loin had said just that. In front of 185 nations gathered at the UN Human Rights Commission (UNHRC) in Geneva, he had told Bhutta where she got off. "You, of all people, have no right to lecture to us about human rights. We know you. I knew your father. I have even had dinner at your place. Your mother is a good cook. Never could I have imagined that you, a little girl whom I knew in pigtails, braces and spectacles, would grow up to be so vicious and dishonest. Who are you? Know your station in life. When your people hanged your father, you collectively hanged democracy. Your boys have raped our women. Your boys have raped our boys," he frothed in the mouth pointing to Bhutta sitting 38 places to his left. "You are comparing Indians to the Nazis and Kashmir to the Holocaust — this shows you are nothing more than a buck-toothed schoolgirl." The Loin had struck.

"The world will not be fooled. You are a nation of rapists," he snarled, as Indian diplomats ducked for cover and the chairman of the UNHRC brought down the gavel in what must have been the fastest flick of the wrist in modern history. Undeterred, the Loin continued till the ambassador sitting next to him whispered something into his ear. Three minutes were up. The Loin had done his number. The Indian exchequer had lost a few.

Every year the Loin travelled to Geneva to tell the world over six tedious weeks that Kashmir was India and India was Kashmir and if Kashmir went, India would follow. The sting was in an emotional appeal. For him that meant biting the microphone after spitting into it for three minutes. He made sure that he used the term "my Kashmir" so that doubts didn't remain about proprietary rights. The Kashmir problem, the Loin clarified, was a Western-Pakistan conspiracy, like the war in Bosnia, with Serbia replacing Pakistan in the equation. In fact, every UNHRC session opened with an Indo-Pak spitting match, which other diplomats called "coffee, cigarettes and loo time", before scurrying towards the exit.

But for India, the Loin's three-minute show during the six-week stay (the taxpayers' part was well over crores by now) was worth every spit. For 180 crucial seconds, the Loin would re-incarnate and defend Kashmir better than any Ministry of External Affairs (MEA) spin doctor or Hollywood script writer, complete with tears in his eyes, quivering lips and trembling fingers. And every year his punch line was: "I will defend Kashmir with the last drop of my blood. You have turned my beautiful valley into a killing field. The Almighty is a witness to this." The possessive "my" was in place.

Beyond that, the Loin was clueless. This was a big secret, as was the fact that the pillar of Indian defence on Kashmir could sleep with his eyes open. The Loin's principal interest in Geneva was ornithology which, under the circumstances, acquired new meaning. He spent a good part of his time, at the taxpayers' expense, birdwatching, in full view of the world. "Where is she from, where is she from?" he could be heard asking diplomats to his left and right, sometimes unmindful of the microphone, leading to laughter all around. Diplomats complained in private that his brief attention span was difficult to cope with. With a few glasses of the South

Asian staple (Scotch' n soda) in their veins, stories about the Loin's escapades would pour out. He, the Loin, liked them short, sweet and, if possible, not very intelligent. Questions bored him.

This time, however, things were different. Very different. This was a post-Babri Masjid demolition UNHRC, billed as the mother of all confrontations — short of a war — between India and Pakistan. The line of control had effectively shifted to Switzerland and both sides had mobilised their best men and women. The Loin was the fulcrum, the country's secular face. Sitting next to Mr. Voyager from the BJP (Bharatiya Janata Party, a pro-Hindu party), and surrounded by diplomats from all religions, this was a perfect photo-op of a mini-India, New Delhi asserted. "We are the only multiethnic country in that part of the world", diplomats learnt to say to every Tom, Dick and Paki who compared Kashmir to Bosnia.

But Bhutta had smelt blood. The Babri Masjid, an unused Muslim shrine in Ayodhya, and the professed birthplace of the mythical Indian god Ram, had been reopened by mischievous politicians to fan Hindu-Muslim dissent in the populous and largely illiterate state of Uttar Pradesh. Some fanatic Hindus had literally torn the mosque down with their bare hands leading to widespread riots not only across India but also in neighbouring Pakistan and Bangladesh. Images of Hindu zealots clawing the mosque down had been beamed to every corner of the world. The image was fresh in people's mind as Bhutta asked the United States, the European Union and the Islamic countries to condemn India.

The incident had shamed most Indians. It had also shown up India's hypocritical commitment to secularism.

The government didn't dare rebuild the mosque for fear of losing Hindu votes. And it didn't dare say so in public for fear of losing the Muslim vote bank, as Indian politicians call Muslims in India. This predicament, attained by India after painstakingly piling mess over lies over mess, was succinctly summed up by another member of the Indian delegation, Musulman Rashid Alam, a foreign-educated, suit-wearing, beardless, capless Muslim leader who, in his more pensive moments in Geneva, remarked: "I am sent here only because I am Muslim. And I am expected to say that in India these things don't matter — what a mess." Indian officials mobilised to defend Kashmir in Geneva, who by this time numbered 83, called him the "brainy leader", thereby clearly implying that the Loin was not. It was a foregone conclusion. No one took the Loin seriously in private. But the public in Geneva was told that the saviour of Kashmir had arrived. The image was more important than the reality. Saving face was supreme.

This was Bhutta's year. Clad in a blue *salwar kameez*, her head draped demurely in a white shawl so that the Organisation of Islamic Conference (OIC) would not be offended, she had spoken to the world from the podium in her high-pitched voice. She urged the UN, and also daddy's friends in the United States, to mediate between her country and India in their long-standing conflict over Kashmir. She scoffed at the proposed elections in Kashmir, which, she claimed, like others that had preceded them, were a "sham" and called for a UN resolution condemning India. She then asked the world to back Pakistan's call for a plebiscite that would give Kashmiris the right to self-determination. "Muslims are not safe in India," she squeaked, and pointed to the demolished mosque. She then asked the commission's members to help Kashmir by voting against India.

India's answer to Bhutta was a blue-turbaned, mild-mannered Mohanman Singh, also a Government College, Lahore, graduate, who countered her figures of Indian troops deployed in Kashmir with figures of India's GDP and growth rates. This, said the MEA, was part of a tactic to rattle Pakistan with India's economic potential. There was also a hidden message to the West — hit us and lose our markets. Besides, diplomats were not ready for another three minutes with the Loin. The last time he had bitten the microphone and the sting of his speech had been lost in laughter. Mohanman Singh was a Sikh and a secular Indian, the foreign office argued; yet more evidence — if evidence was needed — that India was a land of a million religions. Mohanman Singh spoke so softly, no one heard him. When they did, it sounded like he was reciting a poem. India may be right, Pakistan may be wrong, but Indian diplomats in Geneva concluded that New Delhi was all set to snatch defeat from the jaws of victory.

But, as happens in most circumstances similar to these, the people in Geneva had no control over what New Delhi was planning. With each passing day, it became clear that New Delhi too was in the dark about what New Delhi was planning. Thus, to save Kashmir in Switzerland several plans were hatched and demolished by Kashmir experts huddled in rooms all across the Indian capital. In addition to the 83 in Geneva, several others flew in and out of the city to assess the developing situation. Indian newspapers were full of reports of "war" in Geneva, and all across the country people kept track of the votes in favour of and against India as they would cricket scores. The situation was tense, so tense, that the Loin agreed to stop playing golf and devote more time to Kashmir. For him that meant pacing the long corridors of the UNHRC, asking all and sundry *"kya ho raha hai?"* (what is happening?). He was rarely briefed — Indian diplomats were afraid he would misunderstand or talk too much, or tell it all to the next lady who caught his fancy. Their worst fear was a weeping Loin. Too often in the past, he had brought tears to his eyes even when it was not absolutely necessary. But, he was the head of the delegation and his presence was of key importance. He had to be humoured, otherwise Kashmir could not be saved.

Five days before the vote, the Loin surprised every Indian diplomat by announcing that he had a plan. For a starter he wanted a mobile phone. "Everbody except me has one", he complained to the Indian ambassador, who gulped. He got one. He then asked for a bullet-proof Mercedes. "I can see some Kashmiri militants trailing me," he whispered. A suitably black car with dark windows appeared, bringing along with it protocol problems. If he got a phone and a car, it was mandatory that every other alternate leader of the delegation be provided these two items. This was not the time to trigger off a diplomatic incident over the size of cars. National honour was at stake. India opened its coffers.

Then, the Loin complained he was getting unfavourable and inadequate coverage in the Indian press and summoned his favourite journalist from the *"Kall of the Valley Times"* who spent three weeks informing his public about the Loin's efforts to save Kashmir. "*Billow-by-billow account de raha hoon*" (I am giving a blow-by-blow account) he told the Loin every morning, assuring him that blow-by-blow versions of the Loin's efforts were being read breathlessly every morning back home where elections had been announced. Loin was ready for Bhutta.

Bhutta had sent her crack diplomats and spies armed with Indian newspaper reports about police atrocities in Kashmir. Pakistani spies from their famed secret service organisation, the ISI (Inter-Services Intelligence), as discreet and efficient as India's own Research and Analysis Wing (RAW) sleuths, cruised the halls of the UN in Geneva looking for other spies. Overnight, the Serpentine bar outside the UNHRC, a large airport-like lounge with black chairs and glass-top tables, became a reference library for documents on the Indo-Pak conflict. It was here that the issue was debated till kingdom come by Kashmiris of all hues and denominations. The ISI was succeeding. Pakistan knew which button to press to make India jump. And India was jumping.

Pakistan told the world India was a police state, Kashmir was a war zone where half a million paramilitary forces target practice on innocent civilians, that Indians are liars and Indian Muslims are bigger liars. They called Musulman Rashid Alam a "rented Muslim" sending the government into paroxyms of wrath, even though it was no secret that "*sarkari* Musulman" or government Muslim is a term commonly attached to Muslim families whose members have been accommodated in the cabinet or appointed as governors of Indian states since independence.

Muslims, observed Pakistan, are threatened in India just as they are in Bosnia — they are treated like slaves by their Hindu masters who occasionally throw a crumb in the form of an official post so that the country looks secular and human. But beneath all that, there are a thousand Babri Masjids, they said. They quoted chapter and verse from Indian newspapers and reports from Indian civil liberties organisations to affirm that India was a dictatorship where there was no freedom of expression or movement. They cautioned the world against being fooled into believing that India was the world's largest democracy with a huge market of 200 million Maruti riders. "Human rights," said Bhutta, "is a dirty word in India", to the thunderous applause of the UNHRC.

The situation was desperate. So stunning was the lady in blue and so sparkling were the diamonds on her fingers that no one dared ask the prime minister how she could make such accusations when in her own country women were half human beings and where minorities were treated like dogs. The UNHRC, like India and Pakistan, had no time for details. It had its own agenda. The Loin sent his golf kit back to India and vowed to double his efforts. That meant six minutes per day.

The resolution circulated by Pakistan hit India and its MEA between the eyes. For years, Indian diplomats' leitmotif was they didn't want to internationalise the Kashmir question. Yet, it is no secret that till recently — and even now — the MEA had been driven by a single point agenda called Pakistan. At the UNHRC, the tail was wagging the dog. As Pakistan mobilised support for itself, India dug its head deeper into the ground. "We will not stoop to their level," the Indians stressed, but did just that. New Delhi pressed panic buttons in Indian embassies all over the world and anybody who could spell Kashmir was despatched to Geneva to be on standby with a mobile telephone in hand. Most of them did just that. They stood by and spoke to their friends and relatives all over the world at Rs. 400 per minute phone calls to say they were saving Kashmir in Geneva.

However, behind the scenes and away from the Loin's ears, the official reaction was somewhat mixed. This came through at the numerous human rights dinners that were held to "catch" votes. Options were split between those Indians who argued to err on the side of reason and those who by now had turned ballistic. The former said the UNHRC was a political forum that did not discuss human rights and that India should not make matters worse by playing Pakistan's game. They also claimed that the UNHRC was an annual mud-slinging forum where the more you shout and shake, the more you were allowed to shout and shake and that Pakistan should be given a long rope with which to do the needful.

Taking on Pakistan at the UNHRC on Pakistan's terms meant stooping to levels that would, in the end, demean all that India had stood for. The reasonable diplomats hastened to clarify that India was a democracy where people voted once every five years, where the press brought governments down and where the judiciary was relatively free. It could have been pointed out that Pakistan was using Indian press reports to back its case suggesting that Indian security forces literally had the Indian and foreign press at their heels. The voice of reason wanted India to say in Geneva that indeed there had been human rights violations in Kashmir, but these were aberrations which were in no way condoned by the state (this was eventually said two years later). That, said the voice of reason, would have taken the wind out of Pakistan's sails. In fact, some people even went to the extent of saying India should co-sponsor Pakistan's resolution and call Bhutta's bluff. There was no doubt in anyone's mind that if a fact-finding mission was sent to both countries, India would emerge the victor.

Unfortunately, reason fell on deaf ears. New Delhi's mind was made up. Hysteria had won, succeeding in placing India on par with Pakistan, and New Delhi announced that it would stoop to any level to save the honour of Kashmir. Pakistan confirmed that it would do the same. It was in Geneva that ISI and RAW agents spent six weeks wondering who belonged to the ISI, who to RAW and who was a double agent. The spy versus spy war became personal, between those who had gone to Government College, Lahore, before "paltition" and after "paltition". Together, they were going to let all their subcontinental complexes hang out.

India then matched "tuth for tuth". It sent a *barat* (a procession) studded with 20 ambassadors mobilised from as far away as Japan, New York, Nairobi and Peru and as near as London, Paris and Brussels so that the regional mix and vote were contained and suitably entertained. An Indian Army general and a nuts-and-bolts spy from the Home Ministry ("counter injurjuncy," he said) joined the ranks of other spies who by this time were so obvious that an MEA joint secretary begged journalists not to blow their wigs off in national and Kashmiri interest. In fact this JS, MEA, Mr. Rover, had been christened OSD by his colleagues to mean "officer searching for a desk". It was not clear to anyone in Geneva and New Delhi what his task was and once when a journalist asked him what he was doing in Geneva, he shot back: "I am with the minister." Actually, he did have a full-time job which was to position himself next to the minister at every occasion and once even argued with a colleague about where he should be seated. When he was not fighting for a chair, he could be seen running towards important Indians to whisper in their ears: "I have done what you asked me to." By the third day it was clear to everyone except Mr. Rover that nothing was ever asked of him.

New Delhi woke up to the menace of Pakistani propaganda with the sting and subtlety of Indian propaganda. Non-governmental organisations (NGOs) paid for by the Government of India sprung out of every corner of the UN in Geneva. One named All Bharat Institute of Non-Aligned Studies (ABINAS), affiliated to the JNU (Jawaharlal Nehru University, New Delhi), for that anti-government ring, was particularly active. Its members gained weight with each passing day and complained in public that the embassy was not providing them with "vehicles" to transport their "dakuments".

In pursuit of the resolution, Pakistan's ISI had unleashed a barrage of papers and photographs showing Indian atrocities in Kashmir and tortured bodies. Indian spies did one better. They produced photographs of headless bodies, claiming that these were victims of Pakistani brutalities. The Serpentine bar was by now full of raped Kashmiris, beaten Kashmiris, tortured Kashmiris, homeless Kashmiris and American Kashmiris. Suddenly Swedes, Finns, Icelanders and the Norwegians (natural bleeding hearts) were asking about Sopore, CRPF, Rashtriya Rifles, PUCL and the degree of independence accorded to India's newly constituted National Human Rights Commission. Iranians, Albanians, Moroccans, Libyans and Saudi Arabians lectured India on the need to respect human rights. Russia told India that transparency and civil and political liberties were good for health and the US said it was not politically smart to frighten small neighbours. "How can a country of India's size be so obsessed with the Kashmir problem?" chief US delegate Feraldine Gerraro asked an Indian journalist. "Madam, this is our version of the O.J. Simpson affair — were it not for the fact that so many have died, it would be equally ridiculous," the hack replied as Gerraro looked stunned.

The world was too small. The Kashmir problem too big. The Loin felt trapped. Everywhere he turned he was confronted with ignorance, he moaned. "This morning the driver forgot my favourite restaurant — what is going on here? Who is in charge?" he asked a joint secretary in the MEA who looked suitably concerned.

The European Union (EU) comprising the original colonisers sent ambassadors to New Delhi and India bent itself backwards to ensure they were well received. In other words, the India of 900 million people was on its knees in front of not just the Western, Eastern and Southern world, but also Togo.

Mrs. Ainowitall's last supper was in honour of Togo. She had heard from sources that Togo was undecided about which way to vote and that could mean loss of Kashmir. She swung into action as only ambitious wives of mediocre diplomats can. She went shopping at the best outlets in Geneva to prepare for the Togo dinner.

"Question doesn't arise," Mrs. Ainowitall said, signalling to the guests that evening to gather around the roaring Loin and listen to his illuminating discourse. "Question doesn't arise about losing rasolution," she affirmed, signalling to the ambassador from Togo to join the group. Togo's vote was the dark horse. India's fate depended on it. Tied to the nation's fate was her husband's Washington posting.

The guest list was drawn up accordingly, with the style and finesse of Indian diplomacy in matters such as these. Mrs. Ainowitall knew exactly how to mix and match. Just like her dress sense — she was among those women who would always overdress and manage to look half naked, just like Indian spies running around the UN, their wigs flying in the air. So, at the crucial Togo-driven dinner there were the important diplomats, the hungry hacks, an assortment of the "white" foreigners, all wanting to save Kashmir and India, a professor of sociology just for that intellectual tingle, and Indian spies. Discreet as ever. In the evening they metamorphosed into human rights researchers from ABINAS. You could smell them a mile away. How? They flattered everyone in the room shamelessly, to their face. To the Loin they said: "You are mother and father of Kashmir."

The dinner was a huge affair, Twenty politicians — one Reddy, one Misra, one Kaul, etc. — who had been flown in along with their favourite journalists in addition to an assortment of wives, mistresses and children were all invited by Mrs. Ainowitall.

The political *barat* from India included one politician from every political party — a gentle mix of Brahmins, Kayasths, scheduled castes, Muslims with beard, Muslims without beard, and women without burqas. The alternate leader of the delegation was Mr. Voyager from the BJP who made it plain as soon as he stepped out of the aircraft that he would not be seen dead with the "*langoor* (a species of monkey) from Kashmir." In fact, even Musulman Rashid Alam disclosed privately that the Loin was an embarrassment but a political necessity. "He doesn't know what's going on in Kashmir — that's why he is here", Alam often said. Loin's ignorance was a source of constant tension. One day Indian officials jumped when they saw him attending a seminar organised by a Jewish lobby which trumpeted that the "Islamic menace was spreading east of Turkey west of Tokyo", a comment to which the Loin was seen vigorously nodding his head in agreement. He had to be virtually torn out of the room and be told that he had walked into the wrong meeting.

To make matters worse, Mr. Voyager refused to sit next to the Loin, rendering the Kashmir problem an excruciating one for the protocol-ridden diplomacy. At the UNHRC, countries are given two places at the desk and two behind. The ambassador found a way out. The early-rising Mr. Voyager would come for the morning sessions. The late-rising Loin would come for the afternoon sessions beginning at 3 p.m. That way everybody would be happy. And seated.

Even Mrs. Ainowitall was up to date with all these intricacies of the Kashmir problem. For her dinner, she had not invited the BJP leader because he didn't eat meat and the ambassador from Togo didn't eat vegetables. The problem was solved. To secure Togo's vote, Mr. Voyager stayed back in his hotel room that evening eating *dal* and rice sent by a Geneva-based arms dealer who, by this time, had also been roped into the act because of his self-proclaimed connections with Iran, Sweden and South Africa, three geographically diverse but critical countries. This was serious business, India stressed. He may be an arms dealer who had robbed the nation of crores and India's Central Bureau of Investigation (CBI) had called him a criminal in Swiss courts, but this was not the time for petty haggling. The issue at hand required that India join hands with all, even criminals, because it was confronted with the mother of all criminals — Pakistan. Journalists who raised the issue were not invited to official dinners and drinking sessions.

So, at the Togo dinner, the Loin was ably assisted by Mr. Reddy from Hyderabad, the third alternate leader (Mr. Voyager refused to spend six weeks at a stretch in Geneva) of the delegation who spent the evening alternating between cursing Muslims and wondering if a car had been sent to fetch his son from the airport. "Muslims should be put in their place, just like the Sikhs", Reddy muttered as he walked towards the dinner table. Mrs. Ainowitall coughed loudly and dropped her plate hoping to drown Mr. Reddy's voice. Though very Hindu at heart, she wanted Washington at any cost. So she sat Mr. Reddy next to the sound system from where he could be heard telling people how Mrs. Indira Gandhi "solved" the Naxalite problem and had she been there, there would have been no Babri Masjid, no BJP, no Kashmir, no Muslim problem. Suddenly, he got up and walked towards Mrs. Ainowitall to ask if his wife could be taken around shopping in Geneva. "Nothing, nothing, she just wants to see some watches — what is that name huh, Pathak, Pathak something huh?"

"Patek Philippe," Mrs. Ainowitall piped in and looked at the arms dealer who smiled. "Is there anything else your wife would like?" she asked, one eye on Mr. Reddy and the other fixed on the arms dealer. Mrs. Ainowitall had taken over very early in her husband's career and she knew the relative worth of each favour. "IAS *ki beti hoon*", she often said. Her husband was a leg-flapping mathematics graduate from Rae Bareilly (gold medallist, she reminded people periodically) and the only way he could get into the Doon School circles was by abject flattery. Mrs. Ainowitall had made that clear to her husband in no uncertain terms and demonstrated its effectiveness ever since they had married.

"How nice your many rings are — green is my favourite colour too", she told the ambassador from Togo, pointing to the eight gold rings on his ten fingers. She then showed him the gold necklace she was wearing and narrated its history. Her father, also a gold medallist from Government College, Lahore, had given it to her. Along with her husband's gold medal she had melted it (gossip-mongers fuelling the intradiplomat's wives' rivarly clarified there were never any gold medals, hence the melting story) and hesitated, torn between turning it into a Lucknow style *jhumka* and a South Indian style *Kashi Mala*. And then Mrs. Ainowitall, a Hindi film freak, saw Rekha wearing a *mala* that came right down to her waist. That made her mind up. Now she wanted diamond earrings. Her father told her he would gift her a pair if she lost weight. Mrs. Ainowitall narrated all this to the Loin, her 40 guests and the ambassador from Togo in an effort to lighten the air and secure Togo's vote.

"Maybe, I can buy them in Washington," she giggled, throwing that magical word carelessly as she announced dinner, her 52nd and last official meal in six weeks. She summoned her daughter to join the guests and introduced her to everyone in the room as a "topper in her class, just like her father and *nanaji* (maternal grandfather)".

Mrs. Ainowitall's dinner table contained the usual diplomatic fare. *Paneer mattar, malai kofta, pulao,* hot *rotis,* which Mrs. Ainowitall produced by stretching her hands discreetly behind a closed kitchen door, *dal makhani* and the inevitable baked dish — a soggy cauliflower and cheese mess for the foreigners. Mrs. Ainowitall, like most women in her situation, made a lot of food. The dinner was official, so was the bill, and the leftover food would be frozen and consumed for days afterwards. That's how diplomats' wives saved India's money which could then be deployed for Kashmir. National interest was supreme. Outside, every Indian was an ambassador and the lady took her husband's job very seriously.

When coffee arrived, Mrs. Ainowitall asked the ambassador from Togo if he enjoyed the meal. He thought for a while, burped and informed her and the Loin that he had tasted something similar in the Pakistani ambassador's home the previous evening. Mrs. Ainowitall giggled nervously. The Loin trembled. Sensing the tension, Mrs. Ainowitall signalled to her daughter who turned on the volume and the room was drenched in a Hindi film song which Mrs. Ainowitall simultaneously translated for the foreign guests: "What is behind your blouse, what is behind your blouse...?" But, would that secure the clinching vote?

Pakistan required a simple majority of UNHRC's 53 members to censure India. India had worked night and day at each one of those 53 to ensure a negative vote. There were rumours that suitcases had exchanged hands. When confronted with the issue, Indian diplomats said: "What is there. Pakistan is also doing it." Indeed, what they can do, New Delhi can worsen. "Tuth" had been matched by "tuth".

At the Serpentine bar Kashmir dominated. The intelligent interpretation of events had it that the insurgency in the Valley — one of the three regions within the Indian part of the state of Jammu and Kashmir — simmered for many years before it finally exploded in 1990. But before trying to understand why Kashmir caught fire, it might be worth checking the events that led to the state to accede to the Indian Union.

It's fair to say that Kashmir is like no other state in India and its emotional, political and constitutional ties with the country are also very special. The story of India and Kashmir has been told in a thousand different ways by a thousand different people, but the simple story line runs something like this. Hari Singh, its Hindu ruler who held the right to decide its future affiliations when the Indian subcontinent was partitioned in 1947, was reluctant to accede to the Indian Union and if history books and subsequent analysts are to be believed, harboured visions of an independent state, though it remains unclear how he would have sustained a region caught between two feuding countries. It also seems fair to say that it was the

Muslim leadership of the Kashmir Valley which played a key role in deciding that Kashmir would go to India by refusing to align with Pakistan as some kind of automatic calling. It was clear that these Muslims had rejected the religious appeal of an Islamic Pakistan and thrown their destiny with secular India. Any book that you read on the recent troubles in Kashmir will tell you that, paradoxically, the militant movements have touched the chord in the same community (Kashmiri Muslims) which had actively welcomed the Indian Army and cooperated with it to drive out the raiders from Pakistan in 1947.

The explanation for this apparent paradox, Kashmir-watchers say, lies in the fact that Kashmiri Muslims are not only Muslims, they are also Kashmiris and their political fluctuations mirror and sway with the varying forms of threat they perceive either from Pakistan or from India which has systematically failed to see their political and emotional reality. Predominantly Hindu India controls two-thirds of the region called Jammu and Kashmir, its only Muslim-majority state. The remainder, under Pakistan, is known as "Azad Kashmir". The region had once been ruled by Mughals, Afghans, Sikhs and Hindu Dogras before Britain set up a vaguely defined princely state in 1846 to act as a buffer between the Raj to the south and Russia and China to the north. In 1947, Kashmir with its largely Muslim population was expected to go to Pakistan, but Hari Singh faced a revolt in the west and an invasion by Pathan tribesmen from Pakistan; events that sent him bolting into India's arms. In October 1947, he hastily signed an instrument of accession to India in return for military aid, and the territory became a battlefront between India and Pakistan. This famous instrument of accession is the bone of contention between India and Pakistan and both countries run and rerun history to make the point that their version of events is the most accurtate.

Following the failure of bilateral efforts at peace, the Kashmir issue landed in New York at the United Nations Security Council. The UN Council for India and Pakistan, appointed by the Security Council, proposed in its resolution of 13 August 1948 that the future status of Jammu and Kashmir be determined in accordance with the will of the people. India backed the resolution within a week but Pakistan raised a series of objections and evaded its acceptance till 20 December 1948. Views differ, but it is widely believed that Pakistan evaded committing itself to plebiscite (will of the people) for fear of losing it. When they signed, a third of Kashmir was in Pakistan's hands. A second war in 1965 left positions virtually unchanged. The two countries fought a third war in 1971 when East Pakistan broke away to become Bangladesh. Pakistan repeats the "will of the people" line without its preceding words which say plebiscite is predicated on the vacation of the aggression by Pakistan.

Kashmiris' emotional links with the rest of the country have since the beginning been on a roller-coaster and even today Kashmiris say they are going "abroad" when they visit other parts of the country. The instrument of accession, under the India Independence Act, required the rulers of the princely states to cede only three subjects to the Union — defence, foreign affairs and communications. They had the right to frame their own constitutions for the rest. But popular pressure exerted by the freedom movement led to all the states except Jammu and Kashmir surrendering the right to constitution-making to the Constituent Assembly of India. In Jammu and Kashmir the ruler and the political leadership of the state, driven by their own compulsions, insisted on sticking to their original terms of accession. Tensions developed as nationalism for India clashed with similar sentiments for Kashmir over rather clumsy attempts by the former to erode the autonomy of the state guaranteed under a special Article (370) of the Indian Constitution.

The state's history of relations with the Centre has been a painful one, marked by dismissal of elected people's representatives, imprisonment of popular leaders, ballot-box stuffing and, more recently, violence on an unprecedented scale. The people of Kashmir, who had sought protection in India against the threat to their identity and autonomy from Pakistan, have been disillusioned by repeated attempts by New Delhi to ignore or override their sentiments and aspirations.

In 1984, an elected government in Kashmir was dismissed by New Delhi for getting too close to the Congress party's opponents and the same government was promptly installed after it agreed to snap relations with the Opposition and share power with the Congress. The message to the Kashmiris was clear — the Centre, not the people of Kashmir, had a right to choose their government.

Few intelligent Indians will deny that New Delhi has played a key role in driving the state over the edge. Malpractices in local elections, blocking constitutional avenues of protest and disrespect for the Kashmiri identity by New Delhi created the ideal breeding ground for frustration which found expression in militancy, which was aided by arms and training provided by Pakistan. Pakistan's role in exporting terrorism to Kashmir has been documented not only by India but also by independent observers from the European Union and the United States — critical reference points in human rights debates.

There are many in India who say an ideal solution can only be one that satisfies India, Pakistan and the people of Kashmir, and even though Indo-Pak dialogues resume periodically, most of them, analysts say, will have no meaning unless a similar dialogue is initiated between the different ethnic and religious communities within the state so that they can sort out their mutual relations. Pakistan wants a plebiscite now in Kashmir because the conditions are in its favour. India harps on the theme that Kashmir is an internal matter and the rest of the world that matters — the US and Europe — find they cannot lecture to anyone after the mess they have made of Bosnia. In fact, Indian diplomats chuckled in Geneva that Bosnia is the best thing that ever happened to India as that took the pressure off New Delhi to help MITs (Muslims in trouble). It is impossible to get away from the idea that India, above all, has let Kashmir and the Kashmiris down.

Musulman Rashid Alam often told journalists covering the UNHRC battle that "not a single cabinet minister has visited the state to talk to the people...they zip in and out in helicopters and return to Delhi to propose solutions. It's a joke."

It's also a mess and essential to the mess is human rights and the UNHRC. So far away from its original mandate (which itself had become mangled) is this international institution that each year it becomes evident that some humans have more rights than other humans and if you are poor, black and a woman, you have no right at all. It is here that Pakistani NGOs asked for "pulbiscite" in Kashmir. It was here that India went into a tailspin.

The Loin and New Delhi had no time to lose. The Loin ordered that it be ensured immediately that portable telephones carried by the now 83 members of the Indian team were working. Then he ordered that each of them be given a digital diary so that they could look up and call any number in a jiffy. The arms dealer obliged. India was now wired to sound. Then he ordered that food for the whole delegation be brought from homes of diplomats as the last thing Kashmir needed at this juncture was diplomats with diarrhoea resulting from hotel food. That kept the likes of Mrs. Ainowitall breathlessly happy since each had a Washington posting in mind and nothing was more attractive than couching that urge in the national desire to save Kashmir.

In order to ease the strain of work, the Loin had earlier decreed that not only he, but also others, be taken to ski stations in Switzerland every weekend so that they could think calmly, aided by clear mountain air and cow bells. He personally travelled to Gstaad, St. Moritz and Davos. That put the ambassador in a spot. This was March and the budget for the year was up. But Kashmir had to be saved, so India mobilised its war chest. And as the save Kashmir delegation haggled over who got to eat what and who went to Gstaad with the Loin, Pakistan devoted all its time and energy to clinching votes. It unleashed "operation laptop" which comprised sending pretty young things to sit on the laps of potential voters with a view to securing their vote. The ambassador from Togo had been struck by a laptop. Suddenly, beautiful laptops sprung out of the woodwork. Pakistan had struck once again.

India hit back. Its answer to laptops was the "wailing brigade" who could double up as the "raped brigade". They took their roles very seriously. Some of them rolled on the floor reconstituting a rape, while others slammed their foreheads with their fists simulating the death of a son, father or brother. It was all very subtle. The women recounted, through heavily mascaraed eyes, the ignominy of being raped by a "tarrorist" till someone pointed out to one of them that being raped by a non-terrorist was equally harrowing. These women had a special propensity to wail in front of Western diplomats who, caught between a laptop and a wail, preferred a beer. Pakistan spoke about Indian terrorism and self-determination; India pitched for secularism and humanism.

India finally unleashed its secret weapon — the secular humanist. The secular humanist's role was to give the white man a bad conscience by moralising about Bosnia, Afghanistan, Burundi, Chile, Iraq, Iran, Saudi Arabia, etc. The secular humanist's job was to confuse. The secular humanist stood for nothing and everything and could argue for and against everything. The secular humanist was neither a communist nor a capitalist but the uneasy part was that he — it was always a he — looked like you and me and, before you knew it, could convince you that the Kashmiri question is a Pakistani creation.

As the debate raged prior to the big day, it became clear that India's face was more important than Kashmir's future. Anybody who dared attack the situation in Kashmir was labelled an agent of the West. Thus Amnesty International was lying as were Indian civil rights groups like PUCL which, in India's view, was full of frustrated lawyers. India's attitude towards the governments of the US, UK, France, Germany, Japan and Russia was equally subtle — it went from begging for their support to telling them they would not get contracts in India if they backed Pakistan. The US said it would stay out of the debate if India capped its missile programme. New Delhi readily accepted.

But in Geneva, when the world said Sopore, India said Bosnia; when responsible NGOs said Chote Bazar killings, India said Bosnia; and when serious Indian NGOs called for a debate, New Delhi called them CIA agents in league with the KGB and Amnesty International. When Asia Watch, a US-based NGO, which has been unsparing in its criticism of the militants, documented abuses by Indian security forces, the government called them troublemakers working for Pakistan's ISI. The Indian message was clear — go to hell, we don't care about you but we will fight for our right to beg before you.

On the day of the vote, the UNHRC was packed and tense. But a small clutch of Indian diplomats was smiling mysteriously. Just the previous evening it seemed as if all was lost and some Indian newspapers even carried reports saying Pakistan would win the vote by a margin of one.

Now, as the hour drew close, India seemed inexplicably calm.

As soon as order was called, Iran, to the surprise of the entire UNHRC, moved in to say it was mediating between the two countries and Pakistan had decided to withdraw the resolution. Indian diplomats, mobile phones in hand, were seen running out of the room to talk to New Delhi and the arms dealer was allowed to listen to their conversations. It was never clear to anyone what, if any, his role was. But it was clear to everyone that Shia Iran was settling a score with Sunni Pakistan and asserting its influence in the region. New Delhi looked foolish, pathetic and ridiculous as Iran flexed its regional muscle. But back in India, stories of the Indian victory in Geneva was the stuff of front-page reports and lead stories on television and radio.

That evening, the arms dealer held a victory dinner attended by the entire Indian delegation which justified it all by saying that Kashmir had been saved.

As the Loin bade farewell to the Indian diplomats the next day at the Geneva airport, he promised to come back the following year. "Long live Kashmir — long live India," he told the ambassador as the two shook hands.

Back in India, he won an absolute majority in the first state Assembly elections in Jammu and Kashmir since the outbreak of the separatist rebellion. He cried as his National Confusion party demanded greater autonomy for the state and a new golf course.

Kashmir had been saved.

3 / Waiting for GoDOT

*T*ime was when we said you are what you eat. Time is when you say you are how you communicate.

The telecommunications revolution is not about making telephone calls without shouting. It is something much more basic — and frightening — and the lure of dying distance is pushing the world into the throes of an information revolution which many say will be comparable in impact only to the industrial revolution of the 19th century. However, predicting the direction and pace of this change is a mug's game and as Robert E. Allen, the chief executive officer of a telecom giant observed: "If anyone can tell you what the business is going to look five years from now, I want to find out what they have been smoking."

That uncertainty, however, has not deterred international telecommunications companies from preparing for what is turning out to be a shark's game. Governments, under increasing pressure to shed prices and offer better services, are finding themselves no longer in control of rules — now the subject of fierce negotiations at the Geneva-based World Trade Organisation (WTO) — they once scripted and jealously guarded. Information has become an infrastructure sector and how efficiently you communicate will have a direct bearing on *where you stand in the world. Developing countries, eager to make that magical technological leap, now have a myriad mix of possibilities. Each country's winning formula is, however, its own, arrived at by intelligent deregulation that at once spurs the domestic industry as well as invites foreign investment. This meant intelligent choices depending on how far your country was from telecom revolution.*

Once every four years, Geneva is home to Telecom, a giant jamboree for the industry which beckons governments with its state-of-the-art display of ways to wire the world. If you are not present here either as a buyer or a seller, you do not exist in the world of telecommunications — such is the meet's reputation. It is to this crucial meeting that India sends ignorant ministers who stand on the world stage and mumble as if addressing an Indian election rally when much more justice to India and its intelligence could be done by the country's professionals. The result is a devastating read-out that India is still a nation of mumblers who do not know what the telecommunications revolution is all about, Bangalore notwithstanding.

Telecom 1995 was critical for the industry. It was being held two years before Europe deregulated its markets and when a new telecom accord that would wire the world to sound was being hammered out at the WTO. Amidst persistent rumours that the world's telecom giants were scripting the negotiating positions of their respective governments, it was clear to all that among British Telecom, NTT (Japan), Deutsche Telecoms, Unisource and AT&T, the giants were preparing to slaughter each other in their bid to conquer the $1.6 trillion international telecoms market which accounted for 6 per cent of the world's GDP. And this was only the initial assessment of the market potential.

Geneva had taken special care to dress up for the event, expecting a record participation of government and corporate leaders who, for two weeks, would discuss endless market openings and display their wares in a digital extravaganza that was as dazzling as it was blinding. "The poorer you are, the less mistakes you are allowed to make," a spokesperson for the International Telecommunications Union (ITU) organising the bazaar told journalists at the start of the show. Developing countries, she said, were coming to Telecom 1995 as buyers. "Poor countries are looking for the best value for money and this is the best opportunity for them to see what the market has to offer," she added. In addition to business leaders and government officials, some 200,000 people were slated to pass through the fair, a detail that Geneva had noted and pressed into service an impressive array of utilities including special buses, trains and catering services. Every hotel room within driving distance of the city had been booked a year in advance and companies who woke up late — which in telecomese means three years in advance of the next fair — had to resort to flying in their top executives on a daily basis from major European capitals. While Geneva's residents complained, the local authorities were preparing to laugh all the way to the bank — at the last Telecom in 1991 the state was richer by $700 million in two weeks.

The Indian telecommunications minister wanted to dial a revolution. He did not know anything about telecommunications or what it could do to societies, peoples and cultures. That is why he was sent to Telecom 1995. But, unknown to the telecom crowd, he had a clear advantage over other ministers from near-virgin markets like his own. He couldn't read. But he could count. Fast. Legend had it that he could beat a bank clerk, hands down, up or tied. And it was for his counting capacity that he had been hand-picked by the prime minister of India to lead the ministry at this critical juncture as well as the telecom delegation comprising government officials and businessmen to Geneva. When the world said Telecom 1995 was a golden opportunity, the minister said yes. The former referred to the deregulating market. Ministerji had the forthcoming Indian elections in mind. He had a job to do.

Telecom giants spent that fortnight in October 1995 selling their products and global information solutions in a digital extravaganza costing millions of dollars — estimates showed that every dollar spent at Telecom brought five in return. Developing countries like India, least prepared to step into the information era, were asked how many dollars they were willing to spend on telecommunications as a necessary infrastructure *en route* to economic development. "Where is the money?" ministerji snapped and lectured to the CEOs of the telecom world on the virtues of Gandhian austerity and *khadi*. When asked by journalists how India planned to ride the crest of the revolution, ministerji responded: "Everything is very clear in our mind — you come and see for yourself where we are going."

The world, the ITU said, was becoming electronically interdependent. For example, money equal to $2.3 trillion — larger than the economies of most countries — moved through the world's electronic networks every day. And this was just one instance of the increasing flow of electronic information in the form of telephone conversations, fax, electronic mail and television broadcasts. This, the ITU told Telecom 1995, amply illustrated the extent to which the world was becoming dependent on electronic communications which were altering businesses, lifestyles and societies. When asked why telephones in India didn't work, ministerji said that was "Western propaganda" and proceeded to ring his wife in New Delhi on his hand-held set to prove his point. "This," he said, pointing to the slick phone in his hand, "is India's future". The Indian farmer may have his feet in slush and a prayer on his lips for the next meal, but he will have a mobile telephone in his hand. That, said ministerji, was what revolutions were all about.

For several years, telecommunications had been considered a natural government monopoly and where that was not the case, governments eyed competition suspiciously. Most of them complain that the telecommunication explosion raises questions about national sovereignty and national independence but scratch the surface and you will see that the real issue, as everywhere else, is loss of profits. Loss for governments, and profits for companies. Gradually, in some countries and quickly in others, competition was allowed to creep in, but for a healthy industry to flourish, analysts pointed out that it was critical not just to have official acquiescence, but also its willing and unequivocal support. Ministerji was willing to support anything. In fact, he had come to Geneva to tell the world that India was ready for the telecom revolution, prepared to bridge the technological gap between toiling farmers and complaining city-dwellers. In fact, he said, it was time to ignore the cities and take the telephones to the villages. Somebody, it later turned out, had told him that, Sweden had linked all its villages in this fashion. If Sweden could do it, so could India.

One thing, however, is certain. Gone are the days when the telecommunications industry consisted of sleepy utilities serving monopolised markets at inflated rates. Suddenly, distance has died with the result that the cost of making a call is seen by many analysts as the single most important economic force shaping the way societies will henceforth look at themselves and at one another. Deregulated markets would unleash or intensify foreign competition and slash telephone call rates in some 52 countries (not including India) that accounted for more than 80 per cent of international telecom traffic and some 93 per cent of global telecom revenues. New entrants were coming in from all directions, but three trends had already been outlined by companies merging, buying and selling. Some, in anticipation of the global markets, had built networks of their own. Others had found ingenious ways to use infrastructure leased from other businesses and yet others were using cable television systems and wireless spectra. But everywhere, the message was the same — cut prices and expand the range of services, or sink. This was a game where price per line would eat price per line. The consumer would be the ultimate winner. Imagine being able to telephone without losing your voice or cursing your local telephone exchange. Imagine being able to put a call through at the first shot. Imagine a hand-held phone activated by satellites. Some companies at Telecom were already showing off their new technology which would allow communications between hand-held terminals (this could be anything from a telephone to a computer) anywhere in the world. The first satellites designed for this new service, known as global mobile personal communications by satellite, were set to be launched before the end of 1996. Many countries were reluctant to allow satellite handsets past their national boundaries. Millions of consumers, especially in the developing world, said they couldn't wait to subscribe. Technology was overtaking rules.

So, was the future of India in hand-held phones? Unlikely, though Nicholas Negroponte, head of the Massachussets Institute of Technology Media Lab, wrote in his recent book *Being Digital*: "Early in the next millennium, your right and left cufflinks or earrings may communicate with each other by low-orbiting satellites and have more computer power than your personal computer." In India, the mobile cellular phone was still a yuppie-puppie accessory, and even though it had a future in a country wired down by outmoded technology, it was equally clear that it would have to compete with the fixed line telephone as the personal communications device for the mass market.

It was impossible for anyone at Telecom 1995 to predict what would happen five years down the line or what the eventual impact of all this technology and speed would be on societies. For example, Marconi thought radio could be useful mainly for ship-to-shore calls. Trying to predict how societies would change with the telecom revolution is very hazardous. The digital or multimedia revolution was meshing the information technology world and the telecom world in ways that required a thorough re-examination of traditionally disparate rules, styles and cultures. The changes had swept away the remaining distinctions between data processing and telephony and had made it possible for vast amounts of data to be collected, stored, transmitted and manipulated. Telecom 1995 was the hour of reckoning — will everyone in the world have a telephone number where they can be reached? How will society regulate the intrusion of technology into people's lives? How will sovereign governments, their power hemmed in by geography if not history, cope with technology that makes distance irrelevant? It was all about making the right choices given the technology available in the country, ITU told the developing country ministers.

Pitched battles were being fought a mile up the road from Telecom where countries were trying to write rules with the help of the WTO about how to carve up the markets into the next century. The rules required equal treatment of foreign and domestic companies. Fifty-two countries were taking part in the negotiations which had repeatedly fallen at the regulatory fence. The United States which had made firm commitments for market openings was getting restive at the lack of response not just from developing countries but also from the European Union (EU) which was trying to protect the markets of its weaker countries (Spain, Portugal, for example) without jeopardising the interests of its telecom giants and their stake in deregulation. Widely different rules of competition among the 52 countries had led Washington to say that it will insist on a "competition test", a barometer of sorts that would be applied to all companies seeking to offer telecommunication services to see if came up to speed with internationally accepted standards. Several deadlines for a global telecom deal had passed and the US was learning that forcing the pace of change, however desirable, was not going to be easy. The reasons were not far to seek — many countries simply hated the idea of opening up or in some cases dismantling their national monopolies to allow foreign competitors in, especially in the international services area. Washington's biggest worry was that telecommunication monopolies from other countries would rush in and take advantage of low US rates on international routes without offering US carriers equal treatment. Developing countries, said the US, had taken 20 years to reach the levels of competition it currently flaunts and that it would be unfair to accept India, Brazil and Nigeria to offer the same the minute they deregulated. Should no deal be struck by the beginning of 1997 to take effect in 1998, it was clear that many countries would scale their offers down and look for deals between themselves that may not have the stamp of a global trade pact negotiated multilaterally. Analysts, discouraged by successive failed telecom talks, were saying technology will most probably do what negotiators have failed to grasp. They had already started pointing to a host of services — callback, for example — which had got around domestic laws. It was becoming increasingly attractive to telephone India from Europe via the United States, for example, because the rates were a third of the going rates in the respective countries.

Amidst all this excitement every major telecom operator was eyeing India, potentially the world's largest market valued initially at $75 billion. Ministerji knew this. In fact, he had another clear advantage over his counterparts from comparable countries assembled in Geneva to attract investors — he had absolutely no vision for India and no one, just no one, could accuse him of being even distantly futuristic, let alone realistic about India's needs. That meant he would not waste time with unnecessary details like analysing the various offers with a view to securing the best deal for the country. Not for him all this babble about intelligent deregulation. He had a job to do. His prime minister had an election to win.

The ITU was warning that Telecom 1995 coming just before deregulating markets was indeed full of not only opportunities but also pitfalls for developing countries that could be wired to sound as easily as they could find themselves falling between several generations of technology if they opened their markets without thought. At one seminar to discuss opportunities for developing countries ministerji fell asleep. He woke up when the ITU provided the startling information that two-thirds of the world's people had not even made a telephone call in their lives and that the poor countries accounted for only 7 per cent of the world's telephones, a message that was as socially relevant as it was full of potential for the industry. And for ministerji. The problem was that this disparate world was becoming increasingly interdependent (remember globalisation?), and how quickly you could communicate could have a major impact on which globe you would be standing on in the next century, thanks to the tremendously swift expansion of electronic networks every day, a detail that made ministerji's eyes sparkle.

But, from India's point of view, there was no reason to celebrate, at least not yet. India, China, Philippines, Indonesia and Thailand brought up the international rear in the diffusion density of telephones and India was the least ready, the ITU said, to take advantage of a wired world. The country had only 1.1 telephones, five television sets and 0.1 computer per 100 inhabitants. Compared to the United States with 59.5 telephones, 79 television sets and 29.7 computers per 100, India was still in the stone age.

Other facts about India had washed up in Geneva too, including the one that the country did not have a single happy telephone consumer. Telecom types had also facts and figures on their fingertips indicating that the Indian consumer, harassed for decades by inefficient and wasteful government monopolies, would switch to international companies if these could provide reliable services at affordable costs.

Money was central to the debate. India's ambitious attempts at finding a private sector solution to its telecom needs meant walking a tightrope between the kind of service the government claimed it wanted for its people and the sort of returns international telecom operators said they required to come on board. The ITU contended countries like India would have to make judicious choices if they wanted their money's worth. It advised governments to put in place legislation that would incite private investment in telecommunications without bartering away national priorities. The most important thing was to establish a regulatory body that would oversee the process, industry and government, specialists stressed.

The broad rules of the game in India were clear enough for everybody at Telecom 1995. India was too big a market for anyone to handle single-handedly and had been divided into circles. The government asked international companies to combine with big Indian companies to mount a bid. Companies that showed a commitment to rural services and new technology would have a definite edge over breathless capitalists who only wanted to go to Delhi and Bombay — it was important to look socially committed in India, businessmen had been informed.

So was the information that you should look at India's potential with one eye and its politicians with the other to have a complete picture and that you don't have a contract in your pocket if the minister's pockets remain empty. The talk about India didn't concern bribes any more as grease was a part of international business. There was another problem about India and word spread that ministerji did not know what he was talking about, often fell asleep at private meetings with investors and did not know what India needed in the next decade. The big telecom operators waited for hours and days for an appointment with ministerji whose reputation as a bagman for the party in power in New Delhi had preceded him. "The Indian minister, we are briefed, does not know anything about telecom, but he knows there's a lot of money in it," the CEO of a major American telecom company told hacks. "We are told he doesn't talk anything under $50 million and doesn't know a terminal from a television — is that correct?" The joke was on India. Every time ministerji opened his mouth, he drove investors into

China's arms and, by the end of the fortnight, the general conclusions were India's potential was great, but so were its problems and this was a market for those who had the resources and patience for a long haul. India was constantly compared to China where bribe levels are reportedly the same, but political knowledge levels about the country's priorities and possibilities give Western business leaders sleepless nights. "The Chinese politicians know what they want and drive a very hard bargain — forget about ignoring this clause or that through bribes. They take money, but also take what they want," a trade analyst clarified. What was left unsaid about India was disturbing. India had made its mark.

Ministerji was not bothered by these comments. He had not only a mission, but also a message which he delivered at the India Day organised at the Indian pavilion, where true to style, the last planks were being hammered in and the last wires were being pulled even as the first guests started arriving. The pavilion was packed to capacity indicating that the bookmakers had got at least one thing right — India's potential was huge. Ministerji was late and when he arrived 45 minutes behind schedule, clad in a polyester safari suit, white shoes and gold pens popping out of every pocket, he went straight to the podium as silence swept through the room and without any apologies proceeded to read his lines.

"Good evening, ladies and gentlemen. Thank you for coming. Come to India. We have opened everything. Everything has been opened. Nothing is a problem. We have no problem. If you have a problem call me or my secretary. Indiraji had a dream. One village, one television. Dream complete. Rajivji had a dream. One telephone every house. Dream not complete," he said, pausing to clear his throat.

The CEO of a Japanese multinational standing next to a European businessman was heard asking who were "Lajivji" and "Indilaji"? Indian telecom professionals accompanying the minister ducked for cover.

Ministerji was unfazed. "Raoji wants technology jump. India's future, says Raoji, is in cellular phones and teleconferencing. Sit in Delhi and talk to partymen in Bombay, Hyderabad. Save money on air tickets. Save money on food bills in Andhra Bhavan and Maharashtra Bhavan in New Delhi. So, fear not, investors and multinationals, India awaits you with open arms," ministerji declared, stretching his arms out, but not in a begging pose. The Japanese CEO appeared to look quizzical over "Laoji". That nobody understood ministerji was clear. But what nobody could understand was why he didn't use a translator as do the Germans, Chinese, Japanese or French.

"Please collect small gift before you exit," said ministerji as the crowd started dwindling. The gift was a sandalwood elephant chained to a log of sandalwood. Behind the log was scribbled in chalk Rs. 264.80. India had made its mark.

Ministerji had read his lines. There was little point in telling him that subscribers will turn to mobile phones for most of their work only when they cost as much as fixed network rates. There was little point in drawing his attention to figures that showed that penetration for mobile sets in Europe and the United States lagged well behind comparable consumer products such as television sets and video recorders. Ministerji wanted to project the image of a modern, liberalising India under a modern prime minister and a turbaned finance minister. That meant showing his cellular telephone. Besides, it was in importing this technology that his counting capacities would rise to the fore. India, he said, cannot globalise with those ugly black telephone sets. India needed a multi-colour telecommunications revolution.

The ministerji walked out of the Indian pavilion and walked around Telecom 1995 as if in a trance at the Kumbh Mela. He was tired with details about India's options, right choices, wrong technological turns, etc. Indeed, the options for India and the ITU had been repeated at several seminars and meetings that intelligent regulation, not mindless deregulation, was the answer for developing countries. But if things were difficult for India, they were equally difficult for ministerji who felt weighed down by the pressure of the prime ministerial mission, his own ignorance and his cellular telephone. What irritated him most was the long list of major international telecom operators wanting to see him. "What I can do for them," he once snapped when a minor flunky told him India was getting top billing at Telecom 1995 as it had launched a major rehaul of its telecom sectors. "What I can do — tell them to come to Delhi," ministerji reportedly said. Here in Geneva, he had more important things to do and disappeared for several hours every day much to the embarrassment of the Indian delegation. Ministerji's disappearances grew longer and longer and, during these escapades, he switched off his mobile telephone. The official explanation was that he was a heart patient who could not be disturbed. The officious explanation was that he could not be found in his hotel room either.

In his absence, a clutch of telecom ministry officials put up a brave face and attended meeting after meeting where, under normal circumstances, ministerji's presence would have been indispensable. Everybody was talking about the direction of the changes, but the speed at which they would occur was not clear. That pace, industry analysts observed, would be determined not just by technology but also by the interplay of competition and regulation. Competition in telecommunications was important, but this was a strange sort of competition where the new entrant would have to connect to the existing services or be allowed to lay entire networks within which to offer a host of services. If the latter was not possible, then the time had come to discuss the conditions under which new entrants could have access to existing networks. The message was clear. Governments could no longer delay the revolution, nor could they stop it, but with a little bit of intelligence, they could ride the wave.

The Telecom bazaar showed that competitors were offering a mind-boggling mix of related services that included not just telecom companies but also cable television operators, software manufacturers, banks, water companies, railways and many more, all nibbling away at the market. All these brought with them myriad skills and multiple approaches, helping to transform telecommunications from an industry that builds and maintains networks into one that offers communications as an incidental part of a host of other services. India, analysts confirmed, had a solid professional class to take advantage of the changes if only the government would let up a little. But, where was ministerji?

Even though the chief Indian delegate was pitching for cellular phones, professionals were claiming that high costs ensured that the time had not yet come, even in the West, for mobile telephones to displace the fixed telephone as the personal communications medium in the mass market. Conventional wisdom decreed that what India needed the most was the reliable POTS — plain old telephone systems with the "old" to mean a system that had been tried and tested, not obsolete. National priority will not be addressed and money will not be properly invested if too much emphasis is placed on cellular telephones, pagers and multimedia, industry analysts told journalists at a session entitled "Emerging Markets — Opportunities and Priorities." And at the rate of Rs. 17.50 per minute for a mobile telephone, the POTS logic was full of common sense.

When India became independent in 1947, the number of people waiting for telephones was 5 per cent of those who had telephones (80,000). Forty-eight years later, in 1995, the wait-listed persons (2.5 million) are 25 per cent of those who have a phone. In 1947, using a telephone for a year cost, on an average, 2.5 per cent per capita income. It is now 1.5 times, better than the past, but compares poorly with the industrialised West where it is 0.05 per cent. The benefits of POTS, let alone the electronic revolution and multimedia (shorthand for the coming together of the computer, telecommunications and the entertainment industry) had not been passed on to the consumer in India. Yet, ministerji went around Telecom 1995 moralising (what else) that poor Indians were being cheated by bad foreigners. If the Indian consumers were to calculate the number of days their telephones remained out of order or the number of wrong numbers for which they had to pay, the term "rip-off" would have a new definition.

So how was India to invigorate its market, attract foreign investment and protect sectors of its own telecom industry? The ITU said the cake could be cut in three ways — full competition in both infrastructure and services, monopoly in infrastructure and full competition in services and, finally, monopoly in basic infrastructure and services and competition in enhanced and value-added services.

More and more countries were taking the first option as that appeared to lead to faster rates of growth in subscribers, revenues and traffic combined with lower prices and better customer services. But some argued that most people do not need more than one telephone line (or information pathway) into the home or office; therefore, infrastructure competition could duplicate investments leading to oversupply on thick routes where demand and traffic flows are the highest and undersupply on thin routes. In India, for example, prospects for poorer states will be less promising under this arrangement unless an MP from remote places such as Chattisgarh or Kalahandi can pack the punch of 75 other MPs.

The second option — service competition, infrastructure monopoly — has been retained by most European countries on the logic that the network provider carries out common obligations as well as providing universal services at affordable prices. The ITU says this model will work well if the company which provides the infrastructure is separated from the service provider, but few policy-makers are inclined towards this view, preferring instead complicated guidelines to define the connection between the two. The main argument against this model is that few monopolies have managed to achieve universal service. But this arrangement makes customers happy.

Ministerji was not interested in making customers happy and asked a lot of questions about the third option — monopoly in all that is basic, competition in value-added services. This is where the money was.

"But, who is going to pay?" was ministerji's question to all and sundry, leading some unbriefed corporate leaders to assume that this meant he had a thorough understanding of the complicated billing battle which was at the centre of the telecom revolution. The key question to be resolved was whether developing countries, in a free-for-all world, would be allowed to cross-subsidise their services, i.e., use the large incomes that are derived from the earnings on international traffic for subsidising the cost of domestic services? In fact, it was this cross-subsidising capacity that allowed big US companies to achieve their current infrastructure. The cost of a call has nothing to do with what it actually costs and the kill was in the rest — the billing battle was on. The new rules of the game being hammered out at the WTO would have far-ranging consequences for the industry wherein consumers would see the price of international calls fall and that of calling the neighbour go up. But new markets would be opened up for business, and most important from the viewpoint of India, telephones would work.

Ironically, if rates are what they are today, it is because the ITU has fixed them. The organisation's origins are tied to a cartel of some 20 European nations that banded together in 1965 to share revenues from telegraph services. For decades now telephone monopolies and oligopolies, many of them state-owned, have met periodically at the ITU and its predecessors to fix international rates for bilateral revenue-sharing agreements and to act as toll collectors at national boundaries. These tariffs, called "international accounting rates", specify what one operator will pay another to deliver calls to subscribers. In reality, phone companies pay for excess minutes after netting out calls routed through each other's systems. That way everybody gets a share of the market. Estimates of profits for the major operators range from $15 billion to twice that figure but a lot of information about where companies cut costs and what services actually cost is proprietary. What is known is that international telecom traffic is generating some $60 billion annually and is the fastest growing sector of the $500 billion-plus world telecom market. It will come as a shock to governments — some of whom have been siphoning off profits from international phone services for use elsewhere — to see their profits decline, but ponderous and expensive telephone monopolies are a thing of the past.

On the last evening of Telecom 1995, the ITU organised a special seminar to welcome newly deregulating markets and India was the guest of honour. That meant India would have the undivided attention of the entire Telecom world to make its case. An hour before the brainstorming session, ministerji was nowhere to be found. As CEOs, industry analysts, politicians and trade journalists started trickling into the large auditorium, suitably named Arena, the Indian telecom delegation broke into a cold sweat. "He has not even been briefed, he has not even been briefed," an Indian official moaned, flapping his hands in the air while others ran around with their mobile telephones in hand trying to trace ministerji. The Arena started filling up. Laptops were switched on as was the large overhead screen.

The moderator arrived followed by the heads of NTT, Deutsche Telecom, AT&T and British Telecom. They took their seats on the podium five minutes before the session started and twiddled their thumbs (shown up clearly on the overhead screen) as they waited. The chair in the middle was empty, but just a few seconds before the hour, ministerji walked in looking lost. It was time to roll.

"How important sir are the telecommunications negotiations at the WTO for India?" the moderator asked, flagging the debate off. The audience held its breath.

Ministerji looked blank. "Huh? I am not getting your question, please repeat," he said as Indian officials in the audience displayed beginnings of a cringe. "The World Trade Organisation's negotiations on telecommunication, sir, how crucial are they for India?", the question was repeated. Ministerji looked desperate and his discomfiture was captured in minute detail on the large overhead screen. He cleared his throat and said: "I am not understanding question."

To another question on India liberalising its telecom sector, ministerji said: "Everything is open. Everywhere. Actually we don't want to open, but we have been forced to open by vested interests. It is these vested interests that are behind everything — vested interests from foreign only want to make money. We know it and we have no option. Therefore we have taken all steps forward. None backward." India had struck.

The next day Telecom 1995 was over. Swiss newspapers ran stories about how impressed the world was with China, Nigeria, Brazil and the Philippines. There was a box item on India. It said the Indian team left without paying their telephone bills at the Indian pavilion but the Indian delegation had walked away with telephone sets provided for the occasion.

India was ready for the revolution. Ministerji left for London for a holiday paid for by the Indian tax-payer who had also subsidised the Telecom fortnight.

A year later, Indian sleuths discovered $9.7 million in ministerji's house. It is the fault of all these multinationals, he said in his defence. But, of course. As he was taken into custody, he worried about being infected by the dengue epidemic in New Delhi. Multinationals are responsible for that too. But, of course. To suggest anything else would be anti-national.

4 / When Davos Slept...

*E*very winter, a one-street ski station in south-eastern Switzerland called Davos is home to the largest and perhaps the most sophisticated networking bazaar in the world. Officially, it's the annual meeting of the World Economic Forum started in 1971 by a Swiss professor of business administration to provide a meeting point for European businessmen to devise a common strategy to work the international marketplace. But for the participants, it's just "Davos", a word that has become synonymous with some very high-powered networking among corporations, governments and academia, all of whom stop here to pick up business and political trends, float their own, chat, gossip and ski. Over the years, Davos has become the world's largest international bazaar and some 2000 business leaders, politicians, scientists, artists and journalists trudge their way to this rather ugly back-of-beyond Alpine ski station for an annual sojourn to buy anything from ice-cream-vending machines to cars to structural adjustment mantras to ideas, shake the hand that sold a million designer jeans or books or simply sit with the rich and famous and chat about the state of the world. This is where international investors come, hoping to identify new territories, or to track a company that has caught their fancy. Famous academics bounce their mantras off this crowd and artists and writers gather around in a coffee-house-like atmosphere wondering perhaps what they are doing in Davos and share some of their angst with a corporate honcho. The powerful look for glory. Those with glory want to sit next to power. Davos provides each with just the right mix. It's an interesting phenomenon — in Davos everybody is a somebody and nobody at the same time.

The world displays itself at Davos. Indian politicians display their complexes.

When Narahari Rao came to Davos, everybody in the audience slept.

No. That's a slight exaggeration. When the Indian prime minister came to Davos the only people in the audience who did not sleep were those who couldn't. These were Indian officials who would have had no jobs to return to had they been spotted catching forty winks and then there were some forty Indian hacks who filled up the cattle class in the prime minister's plane and pages of Indian newspapers with glorious reports of the prime minister's performance at Davos. "Investors are likely to throng to India...", a leading journalist wrote in an Indian daily while analysing the prime minister's speech at the World Economic Forum.

Narahari Rao and his large retinue (allowed exceptionally, setting aside Davos' no aides rule) came to

Davos looking for investments armed with the country's pre- and post-colonial complexes. He needn't have bothered. By the time he came, those with money to invest had left and the prime minister of the world's largest democracy found himself preaching to the converted. The handful who came into the room hoping to be spurred by Rao to explore investment possibilities in India left the room looking for the Chinese. What was the problem? What do you think? Rao tried to flog some concoction of spiritual capitalism — or was it capital spiritualism — and in the process dealt India a deadly blow as he went through page after page of his speech which ran into 17 long pages. He was preceded by an Indian commerce minister who went around Davos mumbling to the wall and comparing it to an All-India Congress Committee (AICC) session, and followed by a farmer politician from Karnataka who couldn't explain coherently how his state, internationally known for power shortages, proposed to deal with the problem, and another senior politician from Gujarat who smiled a lot but didn't say much. They were joined by a prime minister-in-waiting from Maharashtra who fell victim to his poor communication skills in the world of charm and glamour and insisted on speaking English thus making it clear, once again, that pre- and post-colonial complexes were alive and kicking and that we would rather murder a language than seek the services of an interpreter. Not being able to speak English, however incomprehensible, continues to be an infra-dig of biblical proportions among India's rulers. Our politicians brought with them large, dust-ridden folders on India produced by the government's information department. These extolled the virtues of the land where the Veda and the

World-wide Web co-exist and where pictures of the *Bhangra* (a vigorous Punjabi dance, usually performed by a group) and *Poikal-kudrai* (horse puppeteers from Tamil Nadu)) vied with those of "Brides of India" to show the country's ethnic diversity. In between, there were yellowish photographs of women riding scooters or working in laboratories with masks on their faces. India was modern, but not too much. Its women were progressive, but not too much. You know, a bit of this, a lot of that.

So what is Davos and why is it important?

Views differ, but important people come to Davos because other important people come to Davos. It's unclear how much business actually gets done though businessmen swear it's a great place for an initial charm, body chemistry and a persuasion network that has to be backed by serious negotiations once both sides are seriously engaged. The forum works on the basic principle that international business and political leaders have a premium on their money and time, respectively. Add to this the problem of getting the undivided attention of important people — your own importance in your country notwithstanding — and you begin to understand why more people want to come to Davos than can be accommodated.

So, pressed for time and looking for attention, you come to Davos where you can sign up for dinner and breakfast with your favourite European or Asian prime minister, an American or Chinese politician, tango with a Latin American head of state, charm your way to get a first read of a multibillion dollar business deal you are pursuing or simply discuss objective truth with a Nobel laureate "on the steps or maybe even at the gentleman's", as an English businessman put it. In many ways, it's a very man-to-man world and women come mainly in the category of spouses or to "lighten" the atmosphere and smile admiringly at their husbands when they make a business presentation over dinner to prospective clients. You come to Davos with your spouse and without your power suits (the dress code is sports chic) and pack high business and higher pleasure over a maximum of six days, though most people hit the ski slopes at the end of three days by which time they have distributed all of their 200 visiting cards.

Time is money and money is time and the Davos types know that maxim better than any other. Businesses that are members pay anything between $14,500 to $17,000 in annual dues in addition to $8000 to attend the conference which is by invitation only. It's a businessmen's club and they set the agenda and the pace. Every seller has between three and six minutes to make his point, failing which there are at least a hundred other ideas per square feet floating around. In a world where information and contacts are increasingly seen, and paid for, as indispensable assets, business leaders say what they can pack in Davos in three days is the stuff of several trips round the world and even better — in the latter there's no guarantee you'll meet the politician or the businessman you seek. At the forum businessmen have more than a sporting chance of making the first contact with prime ministers and corporate leaders. However, not everyone looks to the forum as a business opportunity only. Some who feel isolated by their jobs come to Davos to get away from it all, talk about everything and nothing and eventually identify a business partner in Bermuda, Bangalore or Birmingham.

The people's network at Davos works at several levels. Many executives come prepared with detailed lists of people they intend meeting and jobs they want to accomplish. They scout the hallways of the convention centre pausing only to take calls on their cellular telephones or check their stocks in newspapers or on the wires, sip a quick coffee which they make themselves and run again. They find people they want to meet within arm's reach. A book thick enough to give you a backache if you carry it too long lists participants along with their photographs so that you can match face with name. The rest is easy. The bar code on your name tag allows you to send personal messages to a corporate honcho or a Nobel laureate requesting a meeting. The results, businessmen say, are not immediate but, over the years, the network has paved the way for billion-dollar deals, resolved those nitty-gritty business details that can only be washed down with a glass of wine or on a ski slope and, in some cases, even spawned international peace-making.

The forum's organisers take some credit for the easing of relations between East and West Germany in the early nineties. They refer to Hans-Dietrich Genscher, the German foreign minister's famous "Let's give Gorbachev a chance" speech at Davos as the beginning of the end of the Cold War. Greece and Turkey, disclose the forum's organisers, signed a key declaration in Davos to end hostilities and North and South Korea chose Davos as the place to meet for the first time at the ministerial level. It was in Davos that PLO leader Yasser Arafat and Israel's Shimon Peres went through another round of handshakes (in a stirring speech Peres compared the process of peace between Israelis and Palestinians to climbing an Alpine slope in Davos with bare hands) and reportedly discussed autonomy for the Gaza Strip and the West Bank city of Jericho. This is where Pakistani prime minister Benazir Bhutto came to shop, among other things, for submarines and display her nation's Kashmir complex. But Davos is not a big-ticket item politically. Davos is a big showroom where you display your country, your industry, your manufactured goods and your services and try to convince investors why what you are selling is more important than what the prime minister sitting next to you is hawking.

If Davos rarely makes headlines, that's because its organisers say they want it that way. People — excluding Indian politicians — come here to get away from, not seek, publicity. People come here as people, not as personalities and the forum's networking system works, thanks to the absence of interference from flunkies, phones and urgent files. All participants are equal (in terms of importance given to them by the organisers) and rules bar secretaries, aides, captive journalists, spin doctors and speech writers from placing themselves alongside their bosses to inform the rest of the world. Even heads of state are allowed only one aide and one interpreter and a minimum of security personnel who are required to be as discreet as air. The external security is assured by the Swiss who are famous for such drills.

A penny for your thoughts. If you are wondering how our politicians survive in this atmosphere, the answer is simple — they don't. To the Davos forum India sends politicians who are armed not just with their ignorance of Indian and international politics but also with a long list of complexes that can be traced to the days of the Raj in India and beyond. Their message — if India is where it is today — it's because Western imperialists looted us. Before independence it was the British. Post-independence it is a complicated conspiracy between the United States, the World Bank, OBCs, Swiss banks and LDCs and the Italian Mafia. India's version of reality is the most accurate and the rest of the world is out to pervert our way of life. We want investments but we will never cease to warn the world that our history of struggle has turned us into a nation in constant vigil against all forms of cultural perversion. This is what our elected representatives tell us in India. This is what they tell the world in Washington, Paris and New York. This is what we tell the world in Davos.

In fact, nothing is more entertaining than watching our *netas* (leaders) alternate between abject servility, say, in the presence of the World Bank chief to breath-taking arrogance in their dealings with lesser white mortals, most of whom they brush away with disdain. It's power — if you have something to gain, grin. If you have nothing to gain, gripe. No other country in the world views multinationals with such a mixture of dread and envy as Indian politicians do. No other country's politicians beg for money from one side of the mouth while criticising the ways of their donors drom the other; they also add a moral story in the end for good measure. Blaming others and outside forces — multinationals, Western imperialists, the gods, Saturn, karma and the CIA — for every problem in India is a political means, end and pastime for them. They bring this game to Davos. They play it there to pass time because the rest of the world zips past most of them.

The press conferences they call are attended by Indian journalists who have no choice. Davos shows India's leaders up for what they are. The only problem is they don't know that and if anyone dares suggests that the ways of the world have changed, that "anyone" is a stooge of the whites.

Lesson Number One

Indian politicians cannot function without their *chamchas* (flunkies or sycophants). You have noticed this. Most of our elected representatives speak only to their flunkies and the flunkies in return speak only to the minister. This mode of communication has two functions. First, it keeps the dregs at bay. Second, when the minister is incoherent (and this happens quite often), a flunky in the audience typically makes some sense out of it and nervous laughter and relief cut through the durbar which is happy that the minister's incoherence has been drowned in laughter. Of course, in Davos there are no dregs and few people are incoherent but the minister does not know this and continues with his Delhi durbar transplantation efforts. He does this with a clutch of Indian businessmen, some of whom are only too happy to fill the *chamcha*-gap and wastes time and money trying to find out who is attending which dinner in New Delhi, which UP politician has met the prime minister secretly and what that means for his career and which Indian industrialist he has to dine with in Davos so as to ensure investments for his re-election in India.

This feudal Delhi durbar attitude manifests itself physically too. The *neta* will not move from his seat. In

Delhi that has dangerous implications. In Davos where people are expected to go into the hard-sell mode to put their country, business or product forward, the chair-pose is an instant loser. Undeterred, the Indian minister will sit in his chair and will not mingle with the crowd because that is not done in Delhi where he is served not just tea and coffee but also contracts and, if necessary, bank accounts abroad. Tell him Davos works differently and a typical answer is: "Who wants to come to Davos — this is a Western party." Ask them why they are uncomfortable, and true to style they blame the cold, the snow, the jet-lag and the smoke — all part of the Western conspiracy — for their problems.

Lesson Number Two

Indian politicians are not persons. They are politicians first and politicians last. They are former ministers, ministers, or hopefuls, and they carry their political baggage with them wherever they go and expect the rest of the world to ignore that they are simple human beings like the rest of us with two hands, two legs and hopefully a brain. Maybe it is difficult to notice this while sitting in India, but Indian politicians travel abroad, including to a speck on the globe like Davos, without ever leaving India and the prime minister's coat-tails. The joke about the Indian bureaucrat is that if you ask him a question about the insurgency in Kashmir or the Cauvery water dispute, he will talk about his brother-in-law in the Indian Administrative Service who shared a telling detail with him and expect you to be impressed first by the brother-in-law's position in life and later by the detail. The joke about Indian politicians is that very few of them can speak about their country's economy, trade and society with facts, figures and confidence and most of them begin and end every sentence with the words: "As the prime minister was telling me the other day..." and expect the audience to be impressed. Fine by AICC (All-India Congress Committee) standards, but in Davos, where there is a prime minister falling out of every nook and corner, such comments make the world feel sorry for them and Indians sorry for India.

Lesson Number Three

Indian politicians, including those who head important ministries, are clueless about their work. So much of their time in India is devoted to political survival, plotting and subplotting and *Iftaar* and *Akhand Path* diplomacy — time better spent on running the country — that when they meet their counterparts from other parts of the world they have no common subject of interest even though they may be in charge of similar ministries back in their respective countries. Sitting next to an Indian politician at a Davos dinner is an excruciatingly boring experience and Indian dinners are often packed only with other Indian businessmen out to impress the minister who, flunkyless and aideless, is only too happy to discuss Assembly elections in Uttar Pradesh in an Alpine ski resort.

So, very early in the days of India's economic liberalisation, when a commerce minister was asked to explain the country's new trade policy, his automatic reaction was to look for a bureaucrat. Finding none and visibly rattled, he told a Scandinavian minister who had never been to India: "You will notice change all over the country. Please call me when you are in New Delhi," and proceeded to hand out his visiting card which had several scratched and corrected telephone numbers on it. And then the minister let us down once again. Commenting on the manufacturing sector in India he said, "our goods are so good that they are export quality" without realising that India must be the only country in the world that exports the best and provides its own people with inferior quality goods and services. What better indication that we look down on ourselves. But that is not how the minister saw it. For him "export quality" was a sure indication that India was liberalising and globalising. Just before leaving, our minister lectured to the Scandinavian about the *Bhagvad Gita* and told him all gain was the other side of loss. Pointing to the ski slope outside the window as a metaphor for Western decay, he observed that Western industrial societies were hurtling downwards and like downhill skiers who lived dangerously, their economies, by counting time in terms of money, efficiency and speed, had taken the soul out of its timeless existence and traded it in for a bank account. The Scandinavian changed New Delhi for Beijing on his plane ticket.

Lesson Number Four

This lesson is a corollary to the others before it. Indian politicians cannot relax and have a good time because, according to them, having a good time is a dirty Western value that is a direct threat to our ancient Indian culture given to introspective reflection and sublime thought processes. In the minister's travel-now-pay-later vision of religion, where fun is fleeting and suffering is constant, having a good time immediately means something temporal, something fast, something that disappears. When our prime minister falls asleep it is not because he is driven by feudal habits, but because he has gone into deep meditation which helps him remain lucid in this rat race peopled by Western Speedy Gonzales types. The Indian culture has survived only because it has shunned all things speedy and seized the essence of the turn of the karmic wheel. Speed is the enemy of reflection, a virtue the West lost with the industrial revolution. This is our political message for Davos. Our *netas* may be totally debauched in private, but in public and in Davos, invite them for a glass of beer or wine and watch them jump. They will only drink tea during the day (and a soft drink at dinner) and make a virtue out of their complex by telling a foxed president of the German Bundesbank or the head of the Federal Bureau of Investigation (FBI) or the CEO of an Italian multinational, "I am a social drinker" and proceed to extol the virtues of all sorts of abstinence. The bottom line in all this is their vision of a world that the West has money but no morals, and that we in India have all the morals including the moral right to beg from those we despise.

The Last Lesson

An Indian politician is never surprised. He can never look up in wonder and strive to catch the stars for his country. No technological feat is new because it's all in the Vedas; no concept is revolutionary because some Indian saint or seer had written it on a palm leaf hundreds of years ago, and a blind Indian bard had prophesied man would go to the moon even before the Western world knew that such a thing as the moon existed! An Indian politician travelling abroad will reinvent the wheel, in Davos if necessary, because giving credit to others means that our own magnificent historical heritage including Mohenjo-Daro, Harappa and the Golden Age of the Guptas and Cholas would be undervalued.

The obvious question then is: Why do our politicians come to Davos?

Because they feel they have the right to make fools of themselves and India in public and anybody who questions them is either anti-national or a racist. And you cannot tell them the world and civilisation have turned one full circle leaving them behind because their thresholds of shame and decency are determined by AICC sessions. If the civilised world finds our politicians odd, it is because the civilised world is not civilised. We in India have no problem. We are an ancient civilisation which had a fully developed public works department including waterways and toilets while the West was still in the middle ages.

And to Davos we will come and leave our mark as the Indian prime minister did for reasons that Davos is not known for.

The Indian prime minister was very concerned about his security. Ahead of his visit, a crack team was flown in at national expense, of course, to assess the threat and risk factor involved in moving the prime minister from Zurich, where his plane was due to land, to Davos where he was scheduled to speak. After a great deal of thought, discussion and secret messages exchanged between New

WHEN DAVOS SLEPT... | 93

Delhi and Interpol, the Indian crack team (we only send crack teams abroad — crack investigators, crack bureaucrats, crack sleuths, and other cracks) decided that the entire Zurich-Davos route of some 250 kilometres be blocked to traffic while the Indian prime minister's entourage passed — just like all access to South Block in New Delhi is blocked when the prime minister goes to the gentleman's in his office or the airport road in Bangalore is cordoned off every time our prime minister's plane takes off from New Delhi for the two-and-a-half hour flight to the garden city.

This request for closure of access sent the Swiss police and press into splits of laughter. In a country where the president was once not served in a hotel because no one recognised him and where the foreign minister rides a bicycle to the vegetable shop, such a demand was something straight out of an *Asteriks* comic. The Indian sleuths wanted "Z" category protection for the prime minister because they feared the snowman in the Alps was a Sikh terrorist. "I have handled many prime ministers and presidents in my career and to date I have not lost any — what is your record?", the chief of Swiss security asked the Indian team. They called him a racist in private and continued with their demands for "Z" category. The Swiss tried again. They told the team from New Delhi that the Indian prime minister would get as much security as Yasser Arafat and Shimon Peres, among the two most protected men in the world and this, according to them, was the mother of all Z categories.

Won't do, said India and pointed out that PLO plus Israel did not add up to India much less to its Z category and asked with a straight face that all roads that led into the main street in Davos be blocked. The Swiss, struggling to keep a straight face, asserted that would be impossible and the Swiss papers — and the Davos crowd that read them every morning — laughed some more.

Getting people's attention in Davos is a very important thing. And India had certainly succeeded.

5 / Why Does India Buy Almonds from California?

T he Uruguay Round is an attempt to tackle issues of strategic importance for the design and management of the global economy, including the linkages between money, trade and finance. In a number of respects the outcome of the Uruguay Round may vitally affect the domestic development and future of the developing countries.

—South Commission

On 20 September 1986, the Uruguay Round of multilateral trade negotiations was launched at the seaside town of Punta del Este in Uruguay. Eighth under the auspices of the General Agreement on Tariffs and Trade (GATT), the Uruguay Round was billed as the most complicated and ambitious of any post-World War II multilateral negotiations and unlike those that preceded it, the round aimed to go much beyond facilitating transborder trade in goods mainly through tariff cuts and selective lowering of non-tariff barriers. Developing countries, led by a clutch of Indians, questioned the need for a new round and new rules and deeply divisive and acrimonious debates marked the run-up to Punta del Este. It is fair to say that brawns, not brains, Indian and Western, finally pushed India into the negotiations. This is not hindsight wisdom. Even as the round was being launched there were voices in India warning against the dangers of such global ambitions which did not reflect India's ambitions. There were fears that global trading rules would be rewritten in such a way as to further marginalise countries like India, which, at that time, accounted for and, even now, do, under 1 per cent of world trade.

What were those voices of dissent asking then? They were urging the world, including the elite in India, to devote themselves to removing the asymmetry in the international trading system instead of launching a new round and newer rules. It is also fair to claim that for developing countries, the negotiations came down to a full-fledged exercise in damage limitation. Hindsight also bears out their fears that the negotiations were industry-driven and were aimed at reorganising the international economy, institutions and economic relations for the next century. The thrust of the synchronised positions of the United States, the European Union and Japan was to maintain, through the negotiations, an international regime to protect foreign capital and technology and secure compliance. A top European negotiator was clear about it. Chatting with journalists one day, he said the trade talks were political in nature and far from being technical discussions about percentages of tariffs and quotas, the Uruguay Round would sketch the blueprint for trade and economic policies for countries into the next century. He then concluded with remarkable ease that the talks would be a three-way affair among the European Union, the United States and Japan. When asked what that meant for developing countries like India, he replied: "Well, when elephants make love, the *grass beneath is bound to get crushed."* When multilateral pressure on developing countries sometimes failed, bilateral pressure in the form of trade sanctions was used by the US to push countries like India to fall in line. Gains secured bilaterally in this fashion were then multilateralised with the developing world holding the short end of the stick.

The 15 items on the Uruguay Round's agenda were a mix of traditional and new issues. There were, for example, the normal market access for products issues driven by free trade and GATT's basic premise that all barriers to trade should be negotiated away. Then there was agriculture where GATT's free trade rules had not been applied and in the same category fell textiles and clothings, kept out off free trade rules through a series of long- and short-term arrangements that were housed officially in the multifibre arrangement (MFA) and its successive protocols. All these ensured that textile exports of developing countries remained outside GATT rules and away from the world's markets.

Then came certain systemic issues about GATT provisions and their relationship to products and market access. And finally, there were the new issues — trade in services, trade-related intellectual property rights (TRIPS) and trade-related investment measures (TRIMS). TRIPS and TRIMS together with textiles showed up the negotiations' real agenda and confirmed the worst fears among certain sections in India — the rules of the game were being written by the developed countries. The mould was being recast so as to place developing countries in a position even more unfavourable than they were when the negotiations started.

The General Agreement on Tariffs and Trade (GATT) came into being in 1948 as a loose and temporary agreement. It remained as a provisional treaty for 40 years — a contract among governments acceding to it and not a treaty requiring ratification by national governments. Its provisions dealt mainly with the exchange of tariff and trade concessions and there were some clauses that ensured that concessions granted to imported products were not undermined or negated by governmental interference. Post-Uruguay Round, GATT was rechristened the World Trade Organisation (WTO) to reflect its new role and its rule-bound trade regime. Its officials declared officially that, along with the World Bank and the International Monetary Fund, the WTO was going to set the rules of international trade in ways that were bound to provoke changes in a country's international laws and developmental choices. According to Chakravarti Raghavan, an eminent Indian journalist and an authority on trade and development issues, the Uruguay Round would do to the next century what gunboat diplomacy and colonisers did to the last century. In his incisive work, Recolonisation — GATT, the Uruguay Round and the Third World, Raghavan has argued that the efforts of the industrialised countries directed against the developing world and aimed at circumscribing their process of industrialisation and autonomous development are not without parallel. He explains that 18th-century Britain tried to impose its mercantilist system on its North American colonies by ensuring that while the latter served as a source of raw materials and market for British manufacture, it would never usurp the manufacturing function. The American colonies hit back through home-spun flax textiles and later imposed tea duty to break British monopoly trade interests in North America in tea which led to the now famous Boston tea party, setting in motion forces that brought about American independence and the birth of the United States of America. This is a quick glimpse at history, but a telling one. Raghavan further observes: "Nearly

150 years later [Mahatma] Gandhi in India hit at the British through his home-spun khadi movement. The efforts of the US and other industrialised countries, through the instrumentality of the Uruguay Round and the instruments to be fashioned through the new themes, will perhaps in the long term be a repetition of the same 'folly' with the same consequence."

The Uruguay Round was an attempt not to put the clock itself back, but to remake the clock so that developing countries remained constantly behind on the curve of economic and technological progress. The negotiations were launched when the economies of major developed countries were still reeling under recessionary years of the 1980s when every figure showed a slowdown. Politicians and economists in the West did not like what they saw — these growth rates were insufficient to sustain the high standard of living that the people in these countries had got used to. In addition there were constraints of a political and institutional nature — compulsions of the arms race, unwillingness to reduce consumption, rigidity of the wage structure, power of domestic lobbies, etc. — that prevented the developed economies to look for fresh solutions and bring about the structural changes in their economies necessary to stir growth. They therefore decided to resort to external means and the Uruguay Round was thus conceived as a shot in the arm, an external impetus.

In forcing the new round of trade talks on developing countries, the West divided to rule. Among the US, Europe and Japan, they fully exploited the vulnerability of many of the developing countries' economies that either had been hitched to international lending institutions or were in the process of doing so. Worse, some countries found that their debts were not being rescheduled because they were being obdurate in GATT. The industrialised world also found avid followers in the developing countries to sell their ideas. Guns and boats had become redundant.

The Uruguay Round and its single-undertaking treaty provisions are indeed like no other before it. It is a complex set of agreements involving simultaneous negotiations at several levels which, when packaged together, have redefined the rules of international trade. These are the first negotiations in which the target, apart from seeking the opening up of Europe's agriculture markets, was the markets of a dozen or more developed among developing countries including India. In essence, it has been quite a successful attempt to restructure and redraw the rules of the international trading system to make it even more favourable to the interests and concerns of the major trading nations and their companies which can ask domestic laws in any country that are not on par with international ones be scrapped, whether or not this reflects the interests of the country concerned. Some have called this attempt "economic colonisation"; others have referred to it as "recolonisation"; while yet others say this is business as usual. In fact, it is also fair to say that the West acted in its own interest, like all adult and ambitious nations do. But India, too, acted in the West's interests.

Why is the Uruguay Round important for India? First, because India is an economy caught between two stools and, at a time of such indecision and upheaval, signing away the right to take sovereign decisions in areas key to the country's development because of international treaty obligations is a dangerous thing. But, beyond everything, the Uruguay Round is important because it's a single treaty and India, like other countries, has to accept it as a whole and cannot progressively adhere to it as and when it deems itself ready. The Uruguay Round is important because by agreeing to "liberalise" under *pressure and at a pace it cannot cope with, much less assimilate, India has given transnational companies near-sweeping rights to set up shop in the country and be treated like locally owned companies while they work the market to their benefit.* In addition, the Third World's access to technology and related information has narrowed, thanks to new the TRIPS regime that, quite clearly, favours big companies. The basic imbalance with TRIPS — and its biggest problem — is that while it provides protection for intellectual property, there is not much concern shown in the agreement for the users of that property.

The biggest problem from the Indian point of view must clearly be one of trust. Human beings are not numbers in an economy. Food, medicine and access to technology are not equations. The Uruguay Round negotiations lasted for eight years beginning in 1986. Successive governments during this period did not take the country into confidence on issues that were being discussed in Geneva (prior to the coming into being of the World Trade Organisation) — issues that would have an impact not just on the price of medicines and vegetables but also on which globe India would be relegated to by the rule makers of the world. Partly this was because not many people in India knew what was going on and those who blew the whistle were either transferred out of Geneva (as was India's chief negotiator in 1988 because the Americans found him too independent) or labelled anti-national. When information started petering out, it was deciphered for the coutry by a clutch of self-serving bureaucrats who claimed in public that GATT was the best thing that could happen to an economy on the verge of a take-off though it was never sufficiently explained where India was taking off for. In private, some of them complained that the country was being done in.

At the end of the day, the only sphere where India could have registered immediate trade gains was textiles. This was one of the Uruguay Round's most contentious issues, and it finished with the package loaded heavily against Indian exports and the West ensured that it would not release its grip over this annual $250 billion market till 2003. In TRIPS India had a lot to lose. It did. With the acceptance of the text, India has ensured that there would be a substantial increase in the price of medicines in the country. The writing on the wall is clear. Indian firms do not have the resources to compete with multinationals in the field of research. In addition, with this new regime in place, agricultural, horticultural and other biotechnological processes will become patentable. It will have an adverse effect on agricultural research because Indian farmers will be obliged to import, at very high costs, new varieties of seeds for which foreign multinationals would have taken the patents. They will not be allowed to use the products from these seeds for any purpose other than planting.

The honest thing would have been to say that, accounting for less than 1 per cent of world trade, India had no choice. The international trade agenda has been drawn up by countries that rule the marketplace and that for the time being India is not among them. There has never been any attempt to stir up a national debate on what the country's options could be. Maybe after examining all the possibilities, the Indian public would have come to the same conclusion that our bureaucrats and politicians, who think for us, did. Maybe not. But New Delhi told us they had fought for our rights and gone down shooting when that was hardly the case. Indeed, until 1988 India told the world it was an adult nation capable of determining its own interests and defending them. In fact, till the mid-term review of the negotiations, that was India's position. Then all of a sudden in 1989 it turned around and caved in claiming that it was "isolated."

Isolation has not deterred India before. Isolation did not deter India from standing up for its interests at the comprehensive test ban treaty (CTBT) negotiations where New Delhi was under severe pressure. The real story of who writes India's economic script will probably not be known for some years. But the degree of cynicism that marks some of our top bureaucrats can be gauged from a comment that one of India's commerce secretaries, who took part in the Uruguay Round negotiations, made to journalists in Geneva. Commenting on the TRIPS regime, he observed: "This is not good for India. In fact the whole Uruguay Round package is loaded against us. But I would have retired by the time most of it comes into effect, so I am not really concerned. Don't quote me on this."

One of India's best kept secrets is that we import almonds from California while we are unable to export our textiles to the West. No finance or commerce minister has ever been able to explain why this is so. One minister told journalists as an off-the-cuff, but on-the-record, remark in Marrakesh (where the final Uruguay Round accords were signed) that "almonds is an explosive issue — I will not be able to comment on it".

Indeed. India imports almonds because Ronald Reagan had an election to win. No, of course you won't understand all this. How can you? No intelligent human being can understand it, but our trade policy, to a dangerously large extent, is not about intelligent choices for India which straddles high-tech with high poverty. It's about lies, it's about secret deals by a handful of bureaucrats eager to please the United States, Europe or both, and it's about last minute telephone calls to New Delhi from GATT — now the World Trade Organisation (WTO) — after foisting the bogey of Indian isolation on an unsuspecting nation. The next time you hear about a finance or commerce ministry official travelling to Geneva (WTO), Washington (IMF-World Bank) or Singapore to sell India abroad, you would be wise to pay attention to the verb "sell". For sell India they do. Down the drain.

The dictionary — any dictionary — describes trade as the business of buying and selling. Indian negotiators have given that word new meaning which a senior European negotiator at the WTO compared to Mother Teresa: "It looks like Mother Teresa has drafted India's trade script — it says give, give, give till it hurts."

When you read you begin with A, B, C, when you GATT about India you begin with T, T and A — trips, textiles and almonds. Or H&N for *haldi* (turmeric) and *neem*. Don't let New Delhi fool you into believing that the *haldi* and *neem* patents granted to America have come as a surprise. The whistle was blown as early as 1989 but then there was no one to listen. In 1989, our politicians had elections to win and the last thing they had time for was a detail like GATT. And don't believe New Delhi when it claims that it is making an all-out effort to defend India. If that claim rings hollow in substance, it is equally empty in form. For example, for long and critical periods during the negotiations, India's GATT wing in Geneva was headless. Even today, the enormous task of defending such critical issues like textiles, environment, investments, and social clauses has been left to two individuals. Our commerce and finance ministers tell us economic diplomacy has replaced traditional diplomacy and India will rise to the challenge. This is a lot of hot air because there's nothing on the ground to suggest they mean business. While most countries, including those in the developing world (Brazil, for example), coordinate their negotiating positions in Geneva after consulting their commerce, finance and environment ministries, our politicians and their officials in these ministries hardly speak to each other, let alone evolve common positions after deciding what India needs. There is often an intraministry war about postings to Geneva and it is because of one such squabble that the WTO wing in Geneva is painfully understaffed. One environment minister visiting Geneva at the height of the environment debate at the WTO did not even bother to find out what was going on because, according to him "...I have come to address the UN, not waste my time with the WTO". Our politicians therefore have no time to coordinate their efforts on issues as critical as trade let alone evolve common positions after deciding what India needs. How is it that they can station 30 people in Geneva when Pakistan wants a resolution on Kashmir and are unable to mobilise such resources for trade, which, in the long run, is more important for national security and stability than any arms control treaty? Is there a driver in the seat? The list of questions is long but the message is always the same — our leaders deny in public what they say in private. Our leaders are more concerned with garnering support for their re-election than helping India become a respectable trading nation.

Today the prime minister — who calls himself a farmer at every occasion but continues to live like a king — wonders why China attracts so muh investments while India's share is a dismal 26th decimal. He wonders where we went wrong. He only has to look in his own backyard — literally.

Blaming the West is the easiest and the obvious place to begin. The European Union is packed with aggressive and major trading nations (as we would like to be) and history is replete with examples of how countries like Germany, Holland, Portugal, Britain, France and Spain, to name a few, went around colonising and subjugating large parts of the world. Everything was perfectly legal, at least from the standpoint of those who wrote the laws then and these countries saw no reason to conceal their ambitions and used an ever-present military power to string together economic, social and political dominance of the countries they claimed as their own.

The two World Wars changed the equation between the powerful nations but the attitude towards the colonies was reborn in another form where the colonised carried the message forward as if operating on some sort of remote control! Now the West does not need gunboats to subjugate countries like India. All it has to do is to pocket a few Kayasth and Brahmin lobbies in New Delhi and their job is done for them even as they press the buttons from Geneva and New York. And there is a pattern to this surrender.

But before going into that, examine how the Government of India reacts every time it runs into trouble over its international trade commitments. It does two things. First, it denies what has not been said and, second, it blames foreign hands for all its problems. The formula has been applied to the GATT-WTO debate with a variation. A lot of time and breath has been wasted in telling us that India cannot get out of the international trade regime even though no one has suggested that. And since blaming the foreign hand here would be delightful irony, the honours have been passed on to the odd Indian politician, bureaucrat, journalist and non-governmental organisation calling for more transparency in India's trade relations with the world.

From Geneva, where trade accords are negotiated, to Marrakesh, where the Uruguay Round was signed, to New Delhi, where supposedly trade policy is formulated after a careful examinaion of available choices, subplots are erected and demolished with a view to obfuscating the main story. That is because our government and bureaucrats have made major commitments affecting the political economy of India without taking the people of the country into confidence. Therefore when a former Indian commerce secretary's (who sat in on the final days of the negotiations calling them a success for India) retiring gift to the country is an interview in an economic daily to say India had succumbed to US pressure on the question of intellectual property rights protection, you don't know if he is speaking the truth now or wasn't earlier when he, along with the mandarins in New Delhi, argued that the accord was in India's interest. In the interview, the former commerce secretary said India had no choice but to accept the IPR regime being forced on us through special laws enacted in the United States. He was obviously bitten by the retirement bug, a strange affliction that hits our key bureaucrats after the deed is done and before the lights are switched off on their careers. This is what one commerce secretary said after he retired. But look at what a commerce ministry official wrote to the WTO in November 1995. The WTO puts out a daily log of press clippings from around the world. A commerce ministry official sent an article from an Indian newspaper to the WTO press office announcing that an Indian drug had got a US patent. So far so good. But the official wrote in the margin. "This can be cited as an example of how developing countries stand to gain from the TRIPS agreement," a jotting that the WTO forgot to erase! Sycophancy takes all forms, but in the end the TRIPS story is really one of loss of faith where one part of the commerce ministry says one thing and the other part the opposite, and when the country asks for an explanation, we are made to feel like fools.

It is also interesting to note what forms our delusions take. Throughout the negotiations we were told all our options are open and even though we were actively participating in the negotiations, we retained the right to walk out. In reality, India had very few options and the WTO ensured that state of affairs very early in the game. Our leaders and bureaucrats repeated the Western *mantra* that the new, rule-bound trade regime would introduce discipline into the marketplace and its newly fangled Dispute Settlement Body (DSB) would ensure that countries stuck to their rights and obligations. This is a little like telling the domestic help in your house if he or she has any problems, it's a good idea to remember that the Indian Constitution and the International Charter of

Human Rights treat all human beings as equal and free. The DSB is ideal when both partners are equally powerful. It will be less effective, if not ineffective, if a weak trading partner seeks redressal from a poweful trading nation. And instead of being a simple treaty setting rules for transboundary trade, the WTO set the agenda for international trade in such diverse areas as agriculture, pharmaceuticals, investments, services, environment, labour laws and soon even human rights, all interlinked and enmeshed. For example, it is not entirely inconceivable that India may be denied access to a particular technology if a group of Western countries conclude that New Delhi is not doing enough to respect human rights in Kashmir. In return, domestic laws in several key areas will have to be synchronised with international obligations.

The Uruguay Round was different in more ways than one from all the other previous rounds. First, these were trade negotiations in which developing countries did not perceive any interest of their own. Secondly, opening markets in developing countries was a clear objective. The defining moment for the second objective came when the United States trade representative, Carla Hills, asserted she was prepared to "pry open developing country markets with a crowbar" if she had to secure new markets for US companies, a statement that earned her the nickname Cowboy Carla.

There is no running away from the fact that the WTO has joined ranks with the World Bank and the International Monetary Fund to run the rest of the world on behalf of the world's big traders and corporations. Fact is that even though India has provided a trade-weighted reduction of 55 per cent on raw materials, components and capital goods, the United States and the European Union (EU) have returned the favour with only 18 and 22 per cent, respectively. Fact is that when India, under duress imposed by a phone call to the commerce ministry from Geneva, agreed to negotiate substantive norms and standards in intellectual property, the *carrot* was more access for Indian goods (including textiles) in Western markets and the *stick* was US pressure under its domestic Super 301 laws that allow Washington to unilaterally hit countries it considers errant. The carrot was a mirage. The stick is still in use.

Fiction is New Delhi telling the country it was an honest broker for India's interests. Fiction is when it pretends to be helpless against the march of the market forces. Fact is that New Delhi's fiction is exploding in its face. When one of India's leading industrialists feels compelled to inform the Europeans about the likelihood of the Indian prime minister and finance minister serving Kentucky fried chicken for dinner "even though it may not be as delicious as our tandoori chicken", he mirrors popular perceptions of a government that had mortgaged its soul. You didn't know, did you, that in the mid-eighties, when, under US pressure, one tough Indian negotiator (later a Planning Commission member) was sent back to New Delhi, American negotiators joked in private in Geneva that the Indian Government should be sent a million-dollar cheque for calling the ambassador home.

Examine another fiction — that of the intellectual property rights negotiations. Look at the way India succumbed to US pressure on TRIPS. As the story is told in Geneva, it took just a phone call from GATT's highest offices to a certain Kayasth-Brahmin lobby in Delhi for India to change course midstream. When it became clear that in another room, Indian negotiators, following their earlier brief, were giving US negotiators a very hard time, telephone diplomacy took over. Within minutes of that phone call, the minister called the Indian negotiators and changed their brief. We shall never know what really happened. But we know what the price tag looks like.

India's departure from its principled position — that TRIPS cannot be negotiated under GATT — was so unexpected that for months after New Delhi had capitulated in Geneva on 8 April 1989, developing countries were asking why. The day that agreement was reached was christened Black Saturday and a senior Latin American negotiator (who went on to become his country's finance minister) and a close friend of India summed up the débâcle with telling effect: "It will take a long time for India and the rest of us to recover from this, if we can recover at all."

The private commerce ministry explanation for caving in to US pressure was that had India blocked the accord, it would have been put on Washington's list of countries against whom unilateral trade sanctions would be unleashed. Within weeks of India surrendering on TRIPS, the US suspended duty-free treatment on a range of Indian pharmaceutical products. A few weeks later, on 29 May, Washington further terrorised India by placing it in the Super 301* list. That was lifted in 1990, but India found itself on the Special 301* (patents) watch list. New Delhi, once again, had fallen between two stools.

---

* Super 301 and Special 301 are clauses in the US Trade Act that permit the American Government to retaliate against trade laws in other countries which in their view – sometimes proven, sometimes not — harm US exports.

That was in 1989 and the then commerce minister justified the *volte face* by saying India had agreed to go along in good faith as there was no prejudice to the outcome. The same minister told journalists later that India was under severe pressure from the US and the country needed political courage and a *swadeshi* movement [*kamar kasni hogi, kiske paas himmat hai* (rough translation: we have to gird our loins, who has got the courage?) were his exact words] to face the Western onslaught. Neither he nor any of his officials believed then that they could control the intellectual property negotiations but no one stood up to tell the country that the accord was a potentially disastrous one for India.

And a potential disaster it is. The TRIPS agreement places several obligations on India. Although, as a developing country, India had ten years to change its patent laws to synchronise them with the international regime, the government has sought to do so immediately. Don't ask why. India's WTO obligations would require that the government accept product patent applications in agriculture and drugs (and these would be kept in a cold storage, as it were, as the actual patent may be granted after ten years once the Indian Act is modified). Both the Presidential Ordinance and the Bill to modify the Indian Patents Act of 1970 have lapsed and there is increasing pressure on India from Western trading nations to speedily ratify the TRIPS accord.

Of the eight intellectual property rights issues (patents, trade marks, geographical indications, copyrights, neighbouring rights, integrated circuits, industrial designs and trade secrets) discussed between countries, India was under severe pressure in the area of patents in the food, pharmaceutical and chemical sectors. Today, processes, not products, in the pharmaceutical and agricultural research, are patented in India. That means any number of entrepreneurs can make the same product as long as their processes vary. It means that no monopoly strangles the consumers especially those sitting at the bottom of the Indian economic ladder. Under the new obligations, all this will change and henceforth India will grant product and process patents. The new trade deal also requires that India give exclusive marketing rights to transnational companies which may have applied for and got a product patent in any other member country of the WTO. Of course, Indian companies can do the same thing, but the only problem is we are not yet there. The kill is in the "yet". The industry-driven TRIPS deal will sooner rather than later result in monopolies based on imports and companies will be free to charge rates they think the markets can sustain. Markets, as those frequented by elites. A direct consequence would be a big question mark over access to decent health care for a large section of the Indian society. "In the long run we have to privatise health care," a senior Indian bureaucrat said when asked about this. Where will most of us be in that "long run"?

There is more. The meaning of "working a patent" will also change radically. India's current patent laws are said to be among the more enlightened ones in the world because they have a social component in them. That is to say they encourage companies to make money without losing sight of the human being for whose benefit most medical research is done in the first place. In its simplest form, a patent is a benefit given by a state for innovative research by individuals for discovering and spreading knowledge that is beneficial to society. It means the end-user is always in sight. India's patent laws took "working a patent" to mean designing, manufacturing and making available innovations at an affordable price. What was "affordable" was decided from the Indian viewpoint and not from any boardroom in London, Basel or San Francisco. Under what India has agreed to now, merely importing a product and selling it would constitute "working a patent" with no obligation to manufacture in India. What this will mean for the Indian manufacturer is for you to guess. What this will mean for your pocket is also for you to guess with no prizes for the correct answer. There is, however, one problem. Many multinationals complain that they are losing money because of cheating by Indian companies in the pharmaceutical sector and one US industry lobby estimates that American companies lost as much as $2 billion in sales in India in 1995. This allegation is not entirely incorrect though figures vary but you cannot correct one mistake by embracing another. Punish the guilty, but why take the country to task?

TRIPS is also about ethics and owning and controlling living systems and organisms which have their own intrinsic values and life cycles. Remember the mad cow? Remember what happens when societies fail to place limits on what human beings can do with other species? The mad cow was fed dead sheep so that it would give us better meat. Nature designed the cow to be a vegetarian. Corn meal prices were on the increase and so cows were fed cheaper offal. Man turned the animal into a non-vegetarian before further turning it into raw material. Reducing life to raw material — as international trade accords often do — removes all constraints on the exploitation and manipulation of life at which men have become champions and this has been repeatedly shown to be dangerous. Meddling with the laws of nature raises a plethora of fundamental questions which, if unanswered, are bound to hit at the existing social and moral order. It is no accident that the accord excludes from patentability commercial exploitation that runs contrary to public and moral order. Even the editors of the new trade law recognised the implication of unbridled and breathless exploitation of nature. But the commerce ministry did not draw our attention to the fact that by giving in to US pressure on TRIPS, the issue of ownership of plants, animals and even the human species was up for grabs. The US has already set a precedent by allowing patents for mammals and is currently collecting genetic material from diverse communities with the intention of patenting human cell lines. Special 301 requires that India accept US IPRs in all these areas.

It is important to realise that the problems that have now emerged and which are reflected in the international trade accords have their genesis in the dynamics of the negotiations. This is not a package that GATT and WTO officials produced by waving a magic wand. Negotiations had been going on for seven years and all 120 contracting parties (as countries are called) contributed to the evolution of the text. Countries like India have been in a no-win situation from the beginning and there has been a sharp deterioration in their position since the mid-term review of the accords in Montreal in 1989. After this, the

US and the EU hijacked the agenda. What could India have done? Not much. But it could have spoken the truth instead of criticising those who did. We are now told Indian negotiators went down shooting. That is half the story. The other half is how India tried to please Washington and Brussels in turns (Indian negotiators were counting on EU help on TRIPS in return for New Delhi pushing for the WTO, the EU's baby, to replace GATT, among developing countries) and ended up on the wrong side of both. Had New Delhi conceded in public that it had no choice, the story would have been different.

In fact, the Uruguay Round story has been one of fudge and trudge from day one. Critical decisions on contentious issues were postponed or fudged in the best of GATT traditions. Take services as an example. India wanted this subject out of the negotiations because this sector is at an incipient stage of development and needed protection for some time. It was clear as daylight that India would not be able to withstand competition from transnational corporations which are the main service providers in developing countries. It is also important to realise that trade in services is not the same thing as trade in goods. The latter is about fairly uncomplicated rules about goods moving from one country to another, whereas services is another ball-game altogether. It is about the right of establishment in a foreign country whether or not that country requires that service and this could have implications for the development strategy, resource mobilisation, industrial policy, social objectives and even the security of the country. There is also an obvious imbalance in the treatment of labour and capital. There is a specific provision for crossborder movement of capital if that is seen as an essential part of market access commitment or if a special commercial presence is involved. There is, however, no such explicit provision on the movement of persons — an area of "export of expertise" where India had a lot to gain. When New Delhi raised these issues and asked that services be kept out of the talks, a legal fiction was erected to get around pesky countries like India. Ministers, meeting as contracting parties, first launched the negotiations in Punta del Este, Uruguay. Then, as representatives of governments, they adopted a declaration to launch negotiations on trade in services. The same ministers representing the contracting parties were acting, on the one hand, in order to be able to participate in a framework of rights and obligations in the traditional area of trade in goods under GATT. On the other hand, the same persons then participated on a separate track as if it was a different meeting where they were required to take a separate decision. This legal fiction ensured that developing countries could return home to announce that they had managed to keep services at bay. The GATT fact was that they were committed to the entire package as a single undertaking — if you accepted one accord, you accepted the whole. Services were in. India had fallen between two stools, again, with its eyes wide open.

In textiles, the only area where India could have made trade gains in real terms, the battle was pitched, uphill and finished in favour of the West. For over three decades world trade in textiles and clothing was regulated under the multifibre arrangement (MFA), a system whose predecessor arrangements go back to the time when quotas were imposed on developing country exporters like India to give the nascent mills of Lancashire breathing and growing time. The MFA was a derogation from GATT's free trade rules, but the developing world needed the Western markets, however restricted the entry. New Delhi hoped it would win on textiles if it gave in on issues critical to the US. It didn't.

The ten-year phase-out of the MFA began on 1 January 1995 when European, American and other importers transferred 16 per cent of their textiles and clothings trade out of the MFA and rehoused it in the WTO's general rules which, broadly speaking, ban quota arrangements. The second stage is due to start in 1998 when 17 per cent of the trade will be integrated with normal WTO procedures, followed by another 18 per cent in 2001. The remaining 49 per cent will be integrated overnight, in one shot, when the clock strikes 12 on 31 December 2004.

The devil, however, is in the detail, because importing countries are "freeing" items which were not under any quota restrictions to begin with. For example, 25 per cent of Indian imports are outside quota restrictions in the US and 27 per cent in the EU. This means the 16 per cent lifting of restrictions in the first phase has not even begun to touch the restrictions and, along with the 17 per cent in the second phase, only about 6 per cent of the quotas would have been removed in the first four years. For example, in the EU's case, items transferred out of the MFA include jute products, coated and water-proof fabrics, floor coverings, men's suits, ties and ensembles as well as women's petticoats. The US has integrated products such as parachutes and seat belts, making it plain that MFA-like restrictions will remain till the very last minute. The dispute rages and India, the bulk of whose exports will be freed from quota restrictions at the end of the decade, has been hung out to dry.

Look at agriculture, not directly hitting India yet, but where the Western agenda is once more painfully obvious. While there has been significant progress within the general discipline, and countries maintaining import restraints, domestic support and export subsidy have been obliged to reduce them to some extent, substantial portions of these would continue in future. But countries that did not have these measures in the past have been prohibited from introducing them beyond *de minimis* or the very minimum levels. This is patently unfair. What it means is that those who have these measures can continue them at reduced levels while others cannot have recourse to them in the future. What's mine is mine. What's yours is also mine in another form. The agreement is based on the assumption that totally free movement of agricultural products across borders is the ideal condition and that it is desirable for a country to import food from those countries where it may be produced at cheaper rates. This may be valid for most developed countries that have enough foreign exchange at all times but this makes little sense for developing countries who are short of cash most of the time. If they depend on food imports as the only option available, it's like buying a one-way ticket to starvation for their population. In addition, food production has too much social and human compulsions associated with it and cannot be tackled by purely economic considerations. For example, agriculture is not considered a commercial activity in many developing countries and farmers turn to the land because they have nothing else to do and from which they eke out an existence. It will be extremely difficult to harmonise these special characteristics with purely commercial and price considerations. The beggars in New Delhi might not understand that the WTO's agriculture regime is good for them.

The pattern of surrender, you may have noticed, is painfully predictable. First, India agrees to negotiate, stating that the outcome is not prejudiced. The fiction is thus flagged off because everybody knows India goes with the begging bowl to international institutions every year and therefore does not have large manoeuvring margins. The commerce minister or secretary then returns home to announce that we will not surrender even as negotiators are privately working out escape clauses. That calms nerves in India, but that also sets up the surrender phase. When negotiations resume, India caves in, alleging it has been isolated. Then the facts emerge and we discover there was a phone call from the WTO, a message from a bureaucrat, or a signal from a businessman to stand India's position on its head.

From an Indian standpoint, the Uruguay Round was an exercise that had very far-reaching consequences. The writing on the wall was clear — under the new trade regime, the autonomy of developing countries in pursuing their development policies would be seriously compromised unless they withdrew completely from the international economic system which, in view of the social and economic structures of these countries, was not possible.

Let's be frank. Walking out of the talks was never a real option, but telling the truth about it was. However, speaking the truth would have meant blaming not the foreigners or colonisers for India's problems. Speaking the truth would have meant placing responsibility on Indians. That, we have seen, is a very difficult thing to do.

Today, India is being colonised, not from abroad, but from within. Only 5.8 million persons in the country, or 0.6 per cent of the population, might rise above the poverty line because of increased economic growth due to trade opportunities flowing from the Uruguay Round, a United Nations Trade and Development report stated recently. Does this justify the loss of self is a question we will have to ask ourselves. The answers are not easy, because the battle is not between free markets and state enterprises. Competition is what brought us out of the caves. Competition and survival instinct are what spur imaginations and lead to discoveries. But competition that leads to opportunistic behaviour and a cowboy culture can also destroy societies. Enlightened rulers know that and have warned through the ages about the need to understand that not all profitable activities are equally valuable to society and there is need for some direction about choices nations must make.

The "who decides for whom with what effect" debate is back on the table as the momentum gathers for a multilateral deal on investments. India and a group of countries are now being pressured into agreeing to work for enforceable global WTO rules on how they treat foreign investment. There is no denying the usefulness of foreign direct investment (FDI) in a country like India as it leads to inflow of capital, development of technology, etc. However, FDI requires actions by the host country government using a range of strategic and tactical policy instruments and governments are being urged by the UN's trade body not to give these away by accepting multilaterally imposed investment accords and disciplines. While it is known what FDI can do, more study needs to be done about what it "undoes" in the host country. In fact, a controversial WTO report on the subject acknowledges that empirical work done on FDI has not tried to establish a cause-and-effect relationship — does FDI inflow cause greater exports or do expanding exports attract FDI? — but states all the same that it is not important to determine this because more capital inflow means more trade. How this is linked to the indigenous industry and local requirements — critical issues in India with its large industrial base and technical expertise — has also not been addressed by the WTO which is now making what it says is a "compelling" case for a multilateral investment agreement. The West is also pushing for international agreements on labour standards, corruption and competition policy in the face of stiff opposition from developing countries.

The WTO has not done too well in the first two years that it has been around and it has been rather unsuccessful as a negotiating forum. Many observers think the problem is that single sector negotiations — telecommunications, shipping, services — do not offer the trade-off possibilities inherent in a full round. However, the WTO is doing booming business as an arbiter of trade disputes. Till November 1996, 51 trade complaints had been lodged with the WTO, 26 in the first year. That's almost one-third of the number of disputes handled by the WTO's predecessor GATT in its half a century of existence.

Predictably, the biggest traders — the US, EU, Japan and Canada — dominate the docket. The real test of the DSB as a fair-trade policeman will come when the WTO faces a politically sensitive issue, like, for example, the US law (the Helms-Burton law) imposing a second boundary on companies that do business with Cuba.

Talk of a new round has been gently floated by some and aggressively backed by powerful Europeans who stress that a new round should be launched by the end of the century. These are dangerous thoughts because a new round will further compound the inequalities in the international trading system. The only hope for India, given its negotiating history, is that by that time everybody in power now would have retired.

So, we were talking about almonds. The story told by the walls of the GATT building in Geneva has it that a powerful lobby of almond-growing farmers had paid a lot of money for Ronald Reagan's re-election. He promised them new markets. India was on their list. So, somebody phoned a certain A.N. Sharma in New Delhi saying if India's precarious balance of payments (BOP) reached a certain threshold, India should, in American national interest, start importing Californian almonds on a priority basis. The deal was struck and the US negotiators in Geneva spoke very fondly of their Kayasth contact in New Delhi whom they happily christened Almonds Negotiator (A.N.) Sharma.

You can sleep peacefully. Our national interests — and American almonds — are in safe hands.

PS: As this book goes to press, there is a heated debate in the WTO about what the first ministerial meeting of the organisation in Singapore (9-13 December 1996) should commit itself to. Originally, this meeting was planned so that ministers could take stock of how and where international trade had gone or not gone two years after the Uruguay Round had been signed. But original trade scripts have often been rewritten and the Singapore meet is no exception. The industrialised world wants newer issues and stricter laws to be on board and a strong lobby is especially keen about linking international trade to labour standards. There is little point in stating, as a host of countries have, that one cannot have uniform labour standards without first having uniform living standards. The US, backed by Norway and France, is especially insistent that a clear link must be established at the Singapore meeting between the WTO's open trading rules and working conditions. Brussels, or the European Union, is keen on getting discussions going on trade and competition policy or how governments regulate business while Japan and Canada, backed by the EU but not Washington, want investment rules to be a WTO topic. India is opposing the inclusion of new areas and asking instead that the West honour its old promises. Like in textiles, for example, where the world's markets will remain closed for Indian exports till 2005. Remember "in the long run"?

Eight years after telling us TRIPS was good for India and two years after signing the accord, our minister told the gathering in Singapore that there were fears about the adverse effects of this agreement on the prices of pharmaceutical products and agrochemicals: "There is a feeling that the developing countries may have to incur heavy costs in implementing this agreement by way of higher royalty payments, increased administrative costs and possible transnational monopolistic control in some sectors. I would hope that we will collectively find ways and means of addressing these concerns." The minister also produced a long whining sound about textiles and told the world that India "remained deeply concerned about the lack of commercially meaningful integration of textiles and clothing products" and that India was even more deeply concerned "about systematic attempts being made by some of our major trading partners to delink the integration process from liberalisation". In other words, the minister was saying India was not happy with the "heads I win, tails you lose" trade equation that had been foisted on it by the major traders. How does all this tie up with the 1994 euphoria when we were told that the Uruguay Round was good for us?

Now that we have a trade-related intellectual property deal (TRIPS), trade-related investment measures (TRIMS), soon we will have an environment component to international trade laws followed probably by a law that binds trade to labour, should we not have a BRAT? Huh?

BRAT — beggar-related agreement on trade so that India's concerns can be addressed. This has the advantage of working both ways — in Washington where we go with a begging bowl every year and in India where beggars abound...

6 / Intellectwar Singh Paperwala

An Indian intellectual is a very funny man. But he doesn't know it and therefore when you laugh at him he gets very angry and will tell you that your character is full of angularities. Don't worry if you don't understand, our man doesn't either, but he is using fancy words like that because he wants to sound important and, more importantly, intelligent. If you feel very, very lost, then keep a dictionary in your pocket from where you can hurl words from the letters X, Y and Z at him. But beware of one thing — you can never insult an intellectual — he will always find some angularity in your character or in your subconscious to tell you that even though you think he is an idiot, he does not mind it because he knows where you are coming from, where your mother and father came from and why he made it and you didn't. Of course, all this does not make any sense. That's why it is called being intellectual. What? Yes, being intellectual means showing a World Bank equation to a beggar to explain why he will remain hungry that day and the next seven years because that is the time it will take for domestic food production to enter the first circle of the demographic explosion where the beggar currently stands.

India is probably the only democracy in the world where intellectuals wear their brain (at least that's what they tell us it is) on their sleeves. In other parts of the civilised world, thinkers draw attention away from themselves and light-seekers are identified for what they are. In other parts of the world, intellectuals come from all walks and all sections of societies. In India they come from circles so closed and incestuous that ultimately they become irrelevant to the country's needs.

Every year, hundreds of Indian intellectuals travel abroad at official expense to help our diplomats and trade negotiators defend the country. Along with politicians and bureaucrats come intellectuals of every hue and colour defending every imaginable and imagined cause. Crores of rupees are spent on transporting intellectuals to meetings in distant corners of the world but their real contribution to any debate, let alone India, remains a mystery. The mystery, we are told, exists only for fools like you and me who ask stupid questions. Never ask an intellectual what he is doing when it seems to you that he is sleeping or dozing during a panel discussion. An intellectual never sleeps — the eyes may close, but the mind never does so and even when he is in bed with his pyjamas the intellectual is plotting and planning his next foreign trip.

Commenting on Indian intellectuals, a senior visiting Chinese diplomat recently told an Indian diplomat in New Delhi that one Indian intellectual was equal to two Chinese intellectuals. "But two Indian intellectuals are equal to half a Chinese intellectual", an equation that our intellectuals can be expected to debate shortly in Peru.

An Indian intellectual also has a typical dress code. In India it's a shawl made from exotic berry and not from Gurjari. This shawl is draped carelessly over the shoulder and sways from side to side slowly as the intellectual walks. An intellectual's steps are slow and studied, not like a GONGO (government non-governmental organisation) or a journalist who runs around breathlessly. For a thinker, the walk is the message. When abroad, the "brain" wears a sleeveless jacket, not from FabIndia, but from Valentino or Yves St. Laurent. The other stuff is for the GONGO and the journalist.

One such very intelligent person is Intellectwar Singh Paperwala, who, in many ways epitomises the Indian intellectual. Or at least what the West sees of the Indian intellectual. Intellectwar Singh Paperwala is also a very funny man. But like other intellectuals who frequent international seminars, he doesn't know it. This chapter casts new light on such an "intellectual" personality.

M**ost of you have heard of at least one form of harassment. Some of you may have been subjected to one or another manifestation of it in your personal or professional life. You know what sexual harassment, Indian Airline's harassment, official harassment, *doodhwala* (milkman) harassment, professional harassment, father-in-law's harassment and intellectual harassment mean. But, have you heard of paper, or speech, harassment?

Meet Intellectwar Singh Paperwala, former Indian diplomat-turned politician, rejected by his own electorate, and yet a very important man who spends all his time in India planning and plotting how he can slip into the next official delegation going to his favourite watering holes scattered across the world. Indeed, just like journalists, housewives, daily wage labourers, truck drivers and executives, people like Intellectwar Singh Paperwala — alas, he'd say with a sigh, there are not too many left and that the "boys and girls" in the foreign office have gone from bad to worse — too have their favourite watering holes. Only, while the rest of us dregs use functional names like bar, tea-stall, coffee party, *dhaba* and club to describe that special spot, Intellectwar Singh Paperwala calls them conferences, brain-storming sessions, Paris Club Round Table, United Nations' meetings, where, we are told, minds meet. And while most of us pay for our coffee, tea or beer, the intellectual drinks and thinks at the country's expense — literally and in every other way that you can imagine — and will travel half way across the world to save the country.

Oozing charm from every pore, Intellectwar Singh Paperwala will slime his way into delegations leaving for New York, Cartagena, Geneva and Nairobi from where he will ensure that reports are sent to Indian newspapers and followed with phone calls to editors with the last line "...is there anything I can get for you from here?" Intellectwar Singh Paperwala's favourite topics are human rights, disarmament and India's foreign policy in the post-Cold War era, but at a pinch he can think about environment and trade policy because he says it is all the same thing. According to him, if you are intellectual about one thing, you are intellectual about everything. Most of what he says consists of petulant ramblings against unidentified enemies who have ruined him and India and if you get the strange feeling that he has hitched his destiny to the nation's, you are right. But, the subject closest to his heart is books and Intellectwar Singh Paperwala will tell you that a cruel conspiracy has taken him away from the world of letters to that of illiterates on whose bounty he has to depend for travel abroad to think.

Intellectwar Singh Paperwala is at home talking about grand and large subjects like truth, matter, beauty and values — issues that he can debate only in faraway cities because nobody in India understands him. For, make no mistake about it — Intellectwar Singh Paperwala belongs to the days of the cantonments, civil lines and the mall and feels trapped in the Ajmal Khan Road ethos (i.e., crassly consumerist ethos) that has permeated Delhi and become a metaphor for his grief. In fact, this is the story of his life and over the years Intellectwar Singh Paperwala has managed to acquire the great brooding-eyes look to mirror his tortured soul, which, he tells people at seminars, conferences and brain-storming sessions abroad, bleeds for his country. India, like its foreign office, has been ruined by quotas that mix the rich with the intelligent, Byron with buffaloes. Saraswati (knowledge) and Lakshmi (money) don't mix and no amount of quotas can make that match work. If you haven't noted it by now, you should — Intellectwar Singh Paperwala has India's interest in his heart, mind, pocket and gait. That is why he is hardly in the country and, from distant spots, he "intellectualises" about where India went wrong and why he was right about India going wrong even before India knew it was going anywhere.

"Even though I come from a royal family," he said, flapping his legs, "I am a socialist because I believe in basic things — it's when you forget the basics that you become a rowdy," he told bewildered journalists in Geneva where he had displaced himself to lecture to the world about human rights and, of course, intellectual freedom.

Intellectwar Singh Paperwala is a master of self-congratulation, almost coquettishly hidden under complaints and moans to be better revealed. So, like the rest of his clan, when he is not telling you that he is waiting for the prime minister to call him, he is ringing editors in New Delhi and hawking book reviews and begging them to change his mug shot (which he carries with him in his pocket for that you-never-know-when occasion when he may be sitting next to a journalist on a plane) in their newspapers and magazines with a more recent one that makes him look thirty years younger.

So, how does one spot Intellectwar Singh Paperwala in a crowd of 1000 people?

Easy. If you are a journalist, he will be drawn to you like a fly to honey and you will find that you cannot take three steps in any direction without stepping on him. He will hound you with copies of his speeches, suggest leads, second, third and fourth paragraphs and insist you get some comments from the West on his comments about the West. If you think you can shrug him off with a nod of your head, you are mistaken because Intellectwar Singh Paperwala will stick to you like excreta on a blanket till you publish his speech. If you are uncooperative, he will ring your editor and complain, and your editor will ring you back and complain about being harassed by Intellectwar Singh Paperwala.

In fact, there's a pattern to it. Helpful diplomats will tell you they are obliged to peddle Intellectwar Singh Paperwala's speeches out of respect for a former colleague, but inform you in the same breath that you are under no obligation to help them. During one meeting in Geneva, diplomats and journalists had worked out an elaborate system with the sole purpose of avoiding Intellectwar Singh Paperwala who once chased a journalist with his speech waving in his hand. If he wonders whether you have a fax machine at home, your survival instincts should tell you the answer is "no" because hidden behind that innocent question are nineteen speeches each running into twelve pages. Unless, of course, you own a stationery shop and have free and unlimited access to fax paper. Fortunately, Intellectwar Singh Paperwala has not discovered the e-mail presumably because that would make him feel like a typist. Indian intellectuals don't type — they only talk.

If you are a minister, then Intellectwar Singh Paperwala will come towards you in a succession of short and quick steps with a pile of files in his hand and a harried look on his face and ask, "did you get my message, did you get my message?" That way he makes it clear that he can leave messages for the minister instead of the other way around. Public perceptions are always very important for public thinkers and Intellectwar Singh Paperwala is a public thinker above all, devoted entirely to the public cause. It's a very unhealthy relationship — the one between politicians and the likes of Intellectwar Singh Paperwala. They feed on and detest each other.

If you are a bureaucrat, then the only time Intellectwar Singh Paperwala will speak to you is when he wants to find out if you have faxed his speeches to sixteen journalists whose names and numbers he will carry in the same pocket as his mug shot. And if you are a third secretary in an Indian embassy abroad, expect Intellectwar

Singh Paperwala to walk all over you after he hangs his coat over your face.

If you happen to be sitting next to him in a plane you will notice Intellectwar Singh Paperwala deeply engrossed in a book entitled *The Political History of Nagorny-Karabakh and Its Implications for the Indian Constitution*. He will scribble furiously in the margins and shake his head from side to side and top to bottom suggesting that he is digesting the matter and, by the time the plane lands, he would have managed to transfer all his complexes on to you.

When abroad, Intellectwar Singh Paperwala will distinguish himself from other intellectuals by the books he reads. *Did Byron Have Parkinson's Disease?*, *The Contribution of the Rhine River to German Thought and Culture*, and *Was Andre Malraux a Fascist*, are some of the books he needs to consult before telling the world what India needs. Please note that Intellectwar Singh Paperwala will not be caught dead reading an American book because he is convinced the English language is undergoing a process of Americanisation and will spend hours over coffee (paid for by his hosts) asking if this enriches or debases English. Tell him American English is unambiguous and functional and he will lecture to you on the virtues of ambiguity as a necessary tool in the pursuit of intellectual heights.

If none of the above works for you, try this. Intellectwar Singh Paperwala is a harassed man with dishevelled hair and he can be seen running around international conferences, a vindictive pencil in one hand and a pile of files under the other arm. He will pause abruptly, as if struck by an idea, gesticulate to himself (the movement is meant to draw attention), take frantic notes and nod to himself. In a political crowd, Intellectwar Singh Paperwala will not sit next to a politician but will look instead to see if he can spot the editor of a newspaper or some harassed journalist. In international fora, he will avoid Indians. In India, he will avoid Indians.

But, let's start at the very beginning. Intellectwar Singh Paperwala traces his stock to a royal family north of the Vindhyas where his forefathers and mothers served the British before the country became independent. Post-1947, Intellectwar Singh Paperwala was packed off to Cambridge from where, for all practical purposes, he never returned. No, to be fair, his body returned but soul and mind didn't, and when he joined the Indian Foreign Service the search for the perfect mean was complete. Intellectwar Singh Paperwala was at peace. From abroad he could serve India. From India he could serve himself. But the quota-ridden and politicised Indian diplomacy couldn't contain his talents and do justice to his genius. So he made the switch that only beckons the brave — he jumped into Indian politics. As he tells the story to anybody who will listen, his first shock came when he realised that he had to speak in Hindi, the language of the domestics. "People don't speak good English any more. As the Queen once told me during my trip to London...", Intellectwar Singh Paperwala exclaimed. The Indian foreign office people hated him. Intellectwar Singh Paperwala had sensed that but he had crossed the Rubicon and joining politics was his revenge on all those minor forms of life who had ruined his prose and poetry in the foreign office.

One fine spring morning in 1994, Intellectwar Singh Paperwala arrived in Geneva and looked harassed and tortured the moment he stepped off the plane. "These Indians will never learn to queue — that is why we are where we are," he shouted at the third secretary who had been briefed about everything but this. Intellectwar Singh Paperwala complained that as soon as the plane taxied in, people jumped from their seats and rushed to open the overhead lockers and tried to tear each other out to the exit. "We are not civilised, there is no hope when there is no queue," he said stomping out of the airport. Indeed, there was little point in brandishing our cultural heritage, our epics, our engineers, doctors and works of art for as long as we didn't know how to queue, the world would treat us like barbarians. Intellectwar Singh Paperwala had spoken.

To Geneva he had been sent as part of the Indian delegation defending Kashmir (Cashmere, to him) at the United Nations. Pakistan was calling for international sanctions against New Delhi. India was calling Pakistan names and Intellectwar Singh Paperwala was cursing the Indian Foreign Service which had seated him in the second row from where nobody, just nobody, could see that he was engrossed in a book about the mating habits of the tse-tse fly. When informed that he was not leading the delegation and, therefore, would be relegated to the second row behind the foreign minister, his upbringing, he later told journalists, came to his rescue. With his head held high — he was a short man and that posture involved a fair amount of effort on his part — he walked out of the meeting and refused to cooperate with Indian diplomats when they sought his intellectual inputs.

Intellectwar Singh Paperwala had other reasons to be annoyed. His speech had been scheduled for 9 p.m. Geneva time. That would be past midnight in India and he would miss the next day's newspapers. To add insult to injury, he was informed that his time had been shifted to accommodate a Bihari politician who had 90 MPs in his clutches back in New Delhi. Buffaloes, moaned Intellectwar Singh Paperwala, had replaced Byron.

Earlier that evening he sent off the third secretary in the Indian mission to fax advance copies of his speech to editors in India and journalists in Geneva. It was too late for India, but Intellectwar Singh Paperwala rang up journalists in Geneva and drew their attention to what he said were the defining paragraphs of his speech. These paragraphs highlighted the fact that Kashmir was to India what the Lake Districts and Stratford-on-Avon were to the British. If Keats had a house in Hampstead, Intellectwar Singh Paperwala had a house in Pahalgam that had inspired generations of Kashmiris. The amphibian world of the Thames' bargemen, described by numerous writers, could be compared in their joy and pathos only to his own poem "The Shikarewala on the Dal Lake" and he rounded off his defence of Kashmir by saying had Chaucer, Spenser, Pope and Dryden been around, they would have agreed that India had to retain Kashmir because Indians spoke better English than Pakistanis.

When a third secretary pointed out that the speech did not make much sense, Intellectwar Singh Paperwala sighed and said: "The sting, dear boy, is in the detail. The triumph of genius is in the eye of the perceptive observer who can take the small and ordinary things of daily life and turn them into riveting prose that transforms the nation and spell-bounds the United Nations."

Intellectwar Singh Paperwala had saved India in Geneva. He wrote about it in his next column when he returned to India to change shirts before taking off for Cartagena where he was scheduled to speak on the virtues of non-aligned ambiguity. And all at the state's expense.

7 / Globalisation: Is It Truly Global?

Recall the face of the poorest and the weakest man whom you may have seen and ask yourself if the step you contemplate is going to be of any use to him. Will he gain anything by it? Will it restore to him a control over his own life and destiny? In other words, will it lead to self-reliance for the hungry and spiritually starving millions? Then you will find your doubts and your self melting away.

— Mahatma Gandhi

Next time a beggar sticks her hand — poverty and hunger, as you may have heard by now, are feminine — into your car while you wait for the traffic lights to turn green, tell her to stop bawling and globalise, surf the Net and find out what the United Nations, the World Bank and other donor institutions are doing for her. Tell her they are moving heaven and earth to mould the globe into one big happy entity and even though she may be dead and gone before that heaven touches her earth, there's hope for her great-grandchildren's great-grandchildren. If she stares at you looking baffled and stupid, stick the recent UN food declaration into her hand before zipping off.

All statistics show that the rich are getting richer. Is this bad, or is this good, is not as important as asking is this just? Is it right that few people eat ten meals a day while many more eat once in ten days if at all? These are not statistics from the top of a fool's head. Leftists, rightists, realists and every other "ists" in the world will tell you that poverty is on the increase in New York, Sao Paolo, Manila, Paris, Geneva and New Delhi. The recent food summit attended, among others, by prime ministers and presidents from all over the world, concluded that at any given time of the day or night, an estimated 840 million people are living in poverty. Note, poverty, not hunger. Poverty is a way of life, it has its own wretched structure. The world wants to reduce this figure by half by the year 2015. Twenty-two years ago global leaders meeting at one such global summit pledged to place a meal in front of every globe dweller within the decade. Twenty record-food production years later, just 80 million people are eating better.

What is this whining sound about poverty when we are talking about globalisation? Does globalisation mean a redistribution of this globe's riches so that everyone can eat? What is the meaning of globalisation when recent statistics on global unemployment from the International Labour Organisation (ILO) show that one billion people around the world or the globe, or approximately 30 per cent of the entire global workforce, is either unemployed or underemployed in industrialised, industrialising and going-nowhere economies?

If our leaders were smart — what's wrong with wishful thinking — they would wake up and declare that food production, agricultural research, soil conservation and saving the environment are important issues, on par with providing jobs, education and health to the world's people. And this includes the dhobi's daughter and the watchman's son. Already, the effort to supply adequate food to the current 5.5 billion in this world is falling a billion short of the hunger fence. By the year 2005, the world will need to serve eight billion thalis *if all of us including that beggar at the traffic light has to eat one meal a day.*

In a globalising India, beggars are slogans. They make good subjects for black-and-white posters that we send abroad when the globe wants to talk about eradicating this and vaccinating that.

The poor man, like everything else our leaders say, is an election slogan in India. Instead of looking at the country's poor — anything between 300 and 400 million people — before formulating policy, our leaders look to the World Bank and the International Monetary Fund *for signals.* Their attempt is to globalise and, from their semi-literate and illiterate perspectives, they think globalisation is a badge of honour that will be conferred on them if they gawk long enough at both these organisations.

Fortunately and unfortunately for us, not everyone in the world is as ignorant and clueless as our leaders. So while we make a virtue out of our lack of knowledge (you've heard the "I'm a humble farmer" lines), there are a few voices that are beginning to question this breathless pursuit of the market mantra with the query: where is the poor human being in all this? Sentences like "think global, act local" might send some of our industrialists along with their favourite finance and commerce ministers into paroxysms of joy, but even in conservative corners of the Western world, there are signs that people have tired of globalisation since their share of the globe is never able to decide which way the globe should turn.

The question is not whether globalisation is good or bad. In fact, that is in many ways a non-issue. Nobody, not even the United Nations trade body (UNCTAD) which backs developing country-driven trade programmes, denies that the market (and genuine) competition is good, but cautions that it is good only for those who belong to it, understand its rules and have the stomach to play by it. Competition is what got men out of caves, competition is what keeps prices down and quality high, competition is what fires the creative genius and competition is what makes nations advance. But globalisation as we see it today is not about competition. It is about rather successful attempts by a few multinationals to gobble the globe for narrow benefits through a system of tightly knit transactions of goods, services and capital that leaves very little for potential new entrants. It is about the law of the jungle and survival of the fittest, factors against which enlightened leadership can activate a series of national policy instruments and priorities.

What? Did you say that "enlightened leadership" in our country is a contradiction in terms? Must it be that way?

The United Nations (UN) makes the startling revelation that 358 families on this globe are as wealthy as 2.3 billion people who live in other parts of the same globe. Does this equation make any sense? And if you can't make sense out of it, shouldn't you be allowed to question its wisdom and the economic orthodoxy that makes such equations possible? Does it make sense that we still hold summits to eradicate poverty (note — poverty, as opposed to hunger) on the one hand and praise the triumph of capitalism on the other? Triumph over what? If capitalism has triumphed, why do 1.4 billion people live in poverty and an equal number spend anything between eight and 14 hours a day struggling to remain out of that loop of the wretched? How many people do you know live precariously, beginning with the lady who cleans the utensils in your house and the man — or boy — who washes your car?

If you think you are finally able to buy international brands of consumer goods "cheap", here's something to think about. Your shampoo bottle costs Rs. 45, your burger Rs. 30, cooking oil Rs. 50 per litre and milk Rs. 10-15 per litre. It's a rip-off. Nowhere in the world do people pay 45 dollars, francs, marks or pounds for a bottle of shampoo or 10-15 dollars, francs, marks or pounds for a litre of milk. As a percentage of your income, if you want to be on par with the globalising globe, you should pay Rs. 4, 3.50, 4.50 and 1.70, respectively, for the above goods. That is not happening because you are paying prices decided in boardrooms abroad, where money managers base themselves on assessments that have no relation to the Indian reality. As a percentage of their incomes, nobody in the world pays 200,000 dollars, francs, marks or pounds for a car! The relevant question is: How much local inefficiency is being subsidised here?

The next time you drive into the countryside in India, look around and ask the obvious questions: What do people in front of you need? Internet? Shampoos or cheese? Or do you think they would stop begging or staring at you when they can drink tea at will as you do and eat at will as you can? Most people don't ask for the stars. In fact, 80 per cent of the globe — the same lot that has got left out of the globalisation drive — would be very happy with job and food security and access to primary medical facilities. Is this too much to ask? Who will provide this? Governments or corporations? Globalisation is about profits. Governments are about people. In the Western world *governments have globalised with, and not at the expense of, their people. It has been painful, but it has been done. Where did we go wrong? Which globe will we be standing on in the next century if we are led by people who make a virtue out of their stupidity?*

The finance ministry official quivered with joy as he waited, clad in a trademark safari suit and silk scarf, for the delegation from the World Bank and an assortment of Western industrialists to arrive at the reception. He had good reason to be happy. The World Bank had given several million dollars to India earlier that morning at an annual pledging conference in Paris. They (the World Bank officials) told the Indian delegation that if India wanted to be a global player, it would have to slash its budget deficit, deregulate, disinvest in public sector undertakings and do something about infrastructure, in particular the power sector. Not a very tall order considering the depth of India's begging bowl, a World Bank official remarked, admonishing journalists who questioned the bank's recipe. "You have to understand that in these days of global competition and global markets, one does not get anything for nothing — there's no such thing as a free lunch," the official said, leaning over a table to reach for a glass of champagne. "You see, unless you break some eggs, how can you make an omelette?" he asked very knowingly.

Not everything, however, was in the bag for our chief beggar. The official work was behind him, but there was one detail that needed tying up. The detail was his daughter, who had just graduated from Delhi University and was looking for an internship. No, not at the World Bank. How could anyone dare suggest that? She had come with her father to see Paris and the father had brought her along with him to the reception for World Bank officials where he slipped her innocently into every conversation with a nervous laugh.

"Globalisation is my favourite subject. I have learnt so much from papa," the daughter told anyone who cared to listen. She also promised to take the bank chief official's wife shopping when the couple visited Delhi the following week.

Welcome to the Indianisation of globalisation where sycophancy is as useful a tool as poverty. But as the country's account managers rush to globalise, their kin in tow, what is the globe doing? The globe is taking a pause, wondering between breaths if development theories have established any reliable and recognised criteria for determining whether development has, in fact, occurred? The globe is stopping to ask if development can be measured uniquely through internal economic indicators like the rate of return or an individual project or GNP or are these artificial constructions of faith erected by national elites to serve international elites who, in turn, look to national elites for reassurance of their faith? In many parts of the globe, including Paris, development theorists are questioning the usefulness of smart and savvy economic models to curb poverty and ask if it does not make for more economic and common sense to begin with human beings and work upwards instead of the other way round? If globalisation does not help people — not the well-fed elites but the poor and hungry majority whose fundamental needs don't receive genuine global attention — what is its use?

The secret is out. Globalisation is not an end in itself any more and trade pundits even on Wall Street are beginning to subscribe to the view that the arguments for globalisation, once a useful tool to guide policy and spur unimaginative politicians, have been transformed into a vulgar, oversimplified dogma. And, like all dogma, this one too sounds dangerously smart. The problem is that our politicians and money managers don't know this and are "globalising" to keep up with the Jones even after the Jones have moved away. What is the meaning of globalisation and who, or what, is globalising? Can the neo-liberal *mantra* of global markets — rapid liberalisation of trade, capital flows and foreign direct investment and a starkly diminished role of the state —make any sense in countries where half the population has no money to go to any market let alone a global one? Who decides, for whom, with whose money and with what effect? Who pays?

Let's be frank. Globalisation is mostly about spreading corporate power, for corporate profits. Companies, whether they be local or global, are not expected to have bleeding hearts — that is the job of the Red Cross. But while corporations work the market for profit, governments — people we elect — are expected to work the corporations around the country's basic priorities which, in India's case, include food, medicines and clean drinking water. That is the balance, the intelligent tightrope walk between managing people and managing money. We all know today that change is coming fast and from directions few can predict. Just to cite one example: the transformation of the modern international economy by information technology alone has ushered in other changes that are as inevitable as they are unstoppable. But there's a difference between liberalising technology and technological liberalisation. Technological change is not a matter of political choice even when it drives people out of jobs and into the arms of poverty. Trade liberalisation is a political choice and not an international inevitability. There is little evidence to suggest that our politicians understand all this. No, no, there's little evidence to suggest that our politicians have the courage to seize this difference and turn it into a serious negotiating position. For them, globalisation, like povety and the *khadi* cap, is an election slogan, and an alibi for most of them to travel to Geneva, London, New York and Paris, asserting India is a globalising economy that should not be ignored. Ask them which globe and they say "don't be a spoilsport". In foreign lands when our ministers are asked questions like "do telephones work"?, "what about infrastructure"?, etc., they become even more incoherent and blame the bureaucrats, electoral arithmetic and the weather for India's failure to globalise at an international pace. How much simpler things would be if we tell the world, when necessary, that India will globalise where necessary.

So, we were saying that globalisation as we know it today is a lot about corporate power and very little about people power. A careful analysis of material available in the United Nations, corporate projections of market trends, the World Bank and the Organisation for Economic Cooperation and Development (OECD) points to some very interesting patterns. For example, of the 100 largest economies on this globe, more than 50 per cent are companies, not countries. Did you know that General Motors' sales are larger than the gross national product (GNP) of Denmark and that Ford Motor Company brings home more money every year than does South Africa or that Toyota, the Japanese car manufacturer, makes more money than Norway? The good news is that if you are among the world's 200 largest corporations, your combined sales are bigger than the combined economies of all but nine countries. That is to say, some 200 multinationals spin and net more money than 182 countries including the world's largest democracy, which happens to be India. And the dominance of these 200-odd companies over the world economy is steadily growing — from 24.2 per cent of the world's GDP in 1982 to 28.3 per cent in 1996. The bad news is that India is nowhere on this globe. Indian companies are nowhere in this list.

The globalisation-liberalisation *mantra* is based on the premise that the march of the market is inevitable. It is fired by fancy theories that contend that the combined punch of capital mobility, technological progress and heightened market competition is an irresistible force beyond the influence of domestic policy-makers and countries should join the process and benefit from it instead of resisting it. It is based on the conventional wisdom which believes capitalism is about the creation of wealth. Those who defend economic models based on these patterns of production and consumption (and will not answer your questions) swear with their hand on their heart that globalisation will have only beneficial consequences, that a universal marketplace is not only inevitable but also in society's best interests and that the current ways of corporate capitalism are generally constructive and contribute to the wealth of nations and individuals, in that order. Tell them their vision is narrow and painfully defective in its social and political assumptions and you will not be invited to their discussions in Washington, Geneva and New Delhi. Our finance and commerce ministers and also prime ministers, many of whom have neither conventional common sense nor acquired wisdom, take their cue from institutions like the World Bank and its cousins to whom they are quasi-permanently yoked, if not financially, then at least intellectually, or worse still, both. They tell us globalisation is good for us because it will bring more jobs into the country and bring down prices. There's nothing on the ground to back that premise. For example, the top 200 firms' sales add up to more than a fourth of the world's economic activity but they account for less than 25 per cent of the jobs in this world. The number of people these top 200 companies employ is under 20 million which is less than three-fourths of 1 per cent of the world's workforce. These figures are not the result of some communist-environmentalist conspiracy. They are available at the drop of a question. The UNCTAD holds the view that the implications of globalisation for poverty reduction are conjectural and hence a matter of dispute. While the estimated creation of 20 million jobs in the developing countries as a result of exports to developed countries is far from negligible, this sum, nevertheless, amounts to an addition of only between 1 and 2 percentage points to the share of manufacturing in total employment in these countries. When the going gets tough, companies typically raise profits by slashing workers — restructuring is the euphemism for throwing people out — not adding them. Corporate types play with organigrams of their companies replacing squares with rectangles and vice versa to find out why profits are not soaring and which employee is sleeping when he should be working. Tomes have been written recently on the devastation that globalisation and the accompanying downsizing of companies have inflicted on discharged workers and managers and their families, and politicians in the West have are rediscovering the social contract where the bond between the employee and the company is seen as primordial.

Because of liberalising and interdependent markets driven by the interests of the corporate world, "globalisation" is largely made up of transactions of various units of the same corporation sometimes on the same continent. In the developed world, for example, there is considerable competition for intraindustry specialisation. In the developing world, multinationals are often vertically integrated operations in a chain guided by the overall oligopolistic nature of the company. In other words, the centre-periphery models are alive and kicking. In other words, a car or computer manufacturer increases his share of the market by shipping parts of his company to produce in the developing world whether or not that host country's developmental needs can assimilate that implantation, often at the host country's expense.

Developing countries end up using foreign exchange for buying goods and services which do not service the majority of their people, but keep the elites happy and begging for more in the name of the poor. Remember that beggar at the traffic lights?

Trade pundits are also beginning to wonder if globalisation, which is turning into economic concentration, actually brings prices down. For example, in the car industry alone, the world's top five firms account for 60 per cent of world sales. In the electronics sector, the top five firms have more than half of the global sales. And no more than five multinationals account for more than 30 per cent of global sales in airlines, aerospace, steel, oil, personal computers, chemicals and the media. Contrary to popular belief, the price line in all these sectors is not held by the local markets but is driven by international standards, prices and rules — hence your shampoo is so expensive. In addition, the world's major transnational companies — 40,000 parent firms and 250,000 foreign affiliates — which are principally responsible for globalising the economy are all located in the West from where they decide what the liberalisation priorities of India, Brazil and South Africa should be and why it is better for you to use synthetic shampoo instead of *shikakai*. Don't get this wrong. This is not a shampoo versus *shikakai* equation, but more one that asks: all qualities being equal, what can India afford at this point in its economic development? Other figures offer interesting insights into who or what is globalising. The UN's development arm (UNDP) discloses that 358 people on the globe own as much wealth as half the world's population or that 358 people's riches are equal to that of 2.3 billion people.

If technology is one force, the UNCTAD says foreign direct investment (FDI) by transnational corporations and the transnational system of production and international economic transactions is now the most dominant element of the global economy. FDI has long overtaken trade as the most important mechanism of international economic integration which is the other name for globalisation. These are investments by large multinationals and they play an important role not only because FDI is evolving more rapidly than trade-based integration of national economies into an international economy, but also because FDI brings with it a package of benefits other than capital. These include technology, management skills and market networks. But examine the FDI flows. Most companies do not make their resource allocation decisions based on requirements or price signals in the host country. In other words, the cost of the shampoo you buy is decided not by your buying power but by the companies' selling tactics and costs including social costs dictated by another economy where workers can buy what they produce. How many Indian workers can buy the foodstuffs, consumer durables and electronic items they produce? Keep asking.

The question that we should ask our money managers is: is it still possible for India to "globalise" while protecting key development sectors? Can the country globalise, for instance, and maintain at the same time a system of agriculture production that assures food security, as well as retain national control over natural resources and protect domestic service industries against unequal competition? Can India stand up and say it is willing to globalise and integrate into world trade and investments at a pace it can cope with and not be forced into accepting trade regimes forced on it by demands of reciprocity from much stronger economies?

Western companies are indeed investing record amounts in developing countries, but India, the world's largest democracy, also has some 200 million of the world's poorest, and is not among the first ten countries that attract this money. Foreign direct investment soared in 1995 to a record $315 billion internationally. Of this $100 billion went to developing countries, and China alone attracted over $38 billion. India's share was $1.7 billion out of this. Of course, that puts us in a better position than subSaharan Africa and some parts of Latin America but that must bring little solace to our finance ministers and bureaucrats who are awaiting the windfall ever since they opened up the economy in 1991 and told us we were going global and could dare global dreams.

But is FDI all good? Numerous seminars, analyses and reports held in, or coming from, London, New York, Paris and Geneva throughout 1996 show that FDI can indeed be useful to developing countries, but this requires actions by the host country's government using a range of strategic and tactical policy instruments which governments should not throw away in the rush to liberalise. Our pundits and their *chamchas* (sycophants) will tell you that we should globalise because that is how everybody in the world (which world?) has two cars and two microwave ovens. Don't believe them because the West did not globalise before it ensured a set of basics for its people (which have since been chipped away) and which did not include two cars but two square meals a day, education for all at affordable prices, paid holidays and some amount of social security. The cars, the microwave ovens and other gizmos came much later, leading people to marvel and worry at the same time at the fact that Western industrial societies had gone from societies in want to societies at leisure within two generations. A lot of this was achieved by intelligent liberalisation. Western industrial societies, like all intelligent management of peoples and systems of production, protected their industries till they were mature and ready for the world. In the three decades before World War I, protection, whether it be of local industry, goods or capital, was the common trend in the developed world and, in Continental Europe, it was almost a rule. After WW I countries across the Continent developed their industries through an intelligent mix of state control and free enterprise. The 1929 Crash and the Depression in the United States led to a period of corporate regulation and social protection. Across the Atlantic in Europe a system of social protection already existed and a further consensus around this was created between the political parties across the board after World War II to become what is known as social capitalism. Contrary to what you have been told, Europe's welfare states are not broke — at least they are not as broke as the United States. OECD estimates for 1995 show gross public debt in Germany, France and Britain lower than that in the United States, while standards of social protection remain much higher. During the first three post-WW II decades, analysts maintain that Western capitalism including the American model accepted the idea of "corporate citizenship" that served as a glue between the community where workers lived and the corporations which functioned in that surrounding. What people felt was as important as what the shareholders said. Today's intellectuals in business and political circles have rejected this view and its implied social contract on grounds that modern societies should evolve around the needs of companies, machines and money managers, local and global, and not vice versa. They have justified the resultant rupture of the social fibre in the name of globalisation where people are numbers in a vast, faceless production line that has little or no relevance to their lives or societies. The public — you and me — has yet to accept this view of the world, but we don't matter. Our money managers have no time for the public anywhere. In their rush to globalise, they have forgotten about human beings.

A senior member of the US Federal Reserves was asked during a recent visit to Geneva, Brussels and Paris what this magic word "globalisation" had actually done for the world's most powerful country? The questioner — probably a fool in the eyes of the intellectuals — wondered what Europeans would gain by inflicting upon themselves the kind of social turmoil and tensions that Americans are going through because of globalisation? Was there any need for western Europe, which already has a net trade surplus with Asia's tigers and higher living standards than those in the United States, to imitate the American model?

Too bad that our elites were not present to listen to what the American said. According to him, globalisation led to two broad gains. One was strong corporate profits and the other was a vigorous growth in exports. He then went on to say that globalisation may not have caused either because, during the same period, the dollar was dramatically devalued and had forfeited approximately half its value against the Deutschemark and the Japanese yen. In other words, what he was actually saying was that it was perfectly possible that America's export successes and its big rise in corporate profits during the last decade would have happened *without* globalisation. American companies sold more abroad because the dollar was cheap and the corporations that did the selling made a lot of money. This is one explanation of what could have happened. It may not be comprehensive, but it is as real as any other and cannot be brushed away. Instead of examining this, our pundits looked elsewhere, to the Western corporate world leaders for enlightenment. Corporate executives patted each other on the back, raised their own salaries and took holidays abroad, while international institutions, intellectuals and Wall Street types lost no time in touting America's export-led economic engine and produced theories to explain this miracle. Today, trade pundits are saying America's managers have become slaves of business schools' theories and 24-year-olds on Wall Street whose vision of the world does not stretch beyond the next quarter in the financial year which amounts to a grand total of 90 days. This band of people has produced a highly destructive, short-term economic programme based on their version of economics formulated by economists writing about societies that bear little resemblance to today's world. If the West is criticising these *mantras* as unsuitable for their world, can you imagine what it means for the people of Kalahandi? But, our leaders don't know that the Jones' have gone out of business; so we run to Wall Street and the World Bank for advice on how to provide basic infrastructure in Karnataka and Gujarat and how to "alleviate" poverty in Orissa.

Our finance ministry types tell us "globalisation" is bringing the world closer together by making a range of goods, services and finances available to a global market of which we are a part. Do you really believe this? If you do, then examine this fact: two-thirds of the world (the bottom 20 per cent of the rich countries and the bottom 80 per cent of the poor countries which includes India) cannot get jobs in the global factories of these companies, much less afford to buy what they sell. There is increasing evidence that globalisation has intensified competition and spawned inequality within and between nations. The potential prosperity that the globalisation of the economy was to have brought has benefited mainly those who own the capital which, in this case, happens to be transnational corporations. Consider this. The gap between the rich and the poor is widening, not falling, because of globalisation. In 1961, the average per capita income in the least developed countries was just under 10 per cent of that in industrialised countries. By the beginning of this decade, it was down to 5 per cent; in 1996 over a billion people were hungry in the world.

It is no exaggeration to say that globalisation has a pecking order. Just like companies in Paris, London and New York don't have time for the people in Kalahandi, Gorakhpur and Gummidipundi, as the case may be, India's finance and commerce ministers too, in their rush to globalise, have no time for Kalahandi, Gorakhpur and Gummidipundi. Elites everywhere have managed to make their poorer fellow global inhabitants pay for the costs of globalisation, whereas they, on the whole, have gained from it or, at the very least, lost proportionally very little. They profit because a lot of their money is abroad and every time their local currency is devalued, they actually become richer at home and are in a position to consume global prices at global rates in local markets. They are the ones who benefit from dismantling export controls. They are the ones who take advantage of cheap and docile labour at home. They are the ones who, like the minister, understand the least what globalisation is all about and are convinced that this is how everybody in America has two cars and two microwave ovens.

Economic theory in many of the developed countries has been fashioned and promoted on ideological grounds by a close group of economists, intellectuals and policy makers — often linked to the World Bank and the IMF or looking for a job there — who read and quote each other and back their *mantras* with high-tech econometrics and computer models that reduce human beings to equations. The spin on the sin is provided by those economists, intellectuals and journalists in the developing world, many of whom are also looking for a job in the West and therefore tout Western models uncritically. Politicians in India, suspended between semi-literacy and illiteracy, are dazzled by smart solutions and not having any recourse to common sense, apply them breathlessly, whether or not they suit the country's needs. The euphoria and the excitement about globalisation are sustained by the will of those who are involved in it in order to justify the circumstances and trade policies that make them and their friends rich. And it is equally protected by the will to ignore, condemn and criticise those who dare question which globe they are standing on since they have looked everywhere, including under their pillow, but not found the benefits of liberalising markets.

So, what sustains this dogma? The same kind of awe, helplessness and anger which makes millions of people believe in karma and ayatollahs. In fact, in an insightful book by Susan George and Fabrizio Sabelli (*Faith and Credit — The World Bank's Secular Empire*) on the bigotry which accompanies international economic prescriptions backed by the World Bank and the IMF, the authors say you don't argue with the structural adjustment salvation model because you don't argue with god! The central thesis of the book is irreverently poignant. Armed with facts, figures and data, the book contends that the World Bank is a supranational, non-democratic institution which functions very much like the medieval Church. Its predictions often have no basis in reality (the recent mess in Mexico is only one of numerous examples), it has a doctrine, a rigidly structured hierarchy preaching and imposing this global doctrine, and a quasi-religious mode of self-justification. It is like a child asking his mother why, if god is all-powerful, are there hungry children in the world? Don't be stupid. You don't argue with god, the World Bank and the finance minister.

The world's decision makers, who include our finance ministers on the fringe, know that the World Bank has failed to solve basic problems of development. But, ayatollahs, gurus and priests too have failed to bring peace and food to the world; yet there is no dearth of believers. Finance ministers in developing countries are the World Bank's apostles who, mesmerised by the globalisation lingo, ask for more — more money and more *mantras*.

The message sent out by the World Bank, globalisation pundits and by our finance ministers is that there is heaven beyond the pain and poverty cycle of losing by structural adjustment programmes (SAPs) and you cannot ask any questions midway — at least not any that would affect the conclave, lest you want to be called a loony leftist. Many of these unverifiable theories have "succeeded" because between 10 and 40 per cent of a country's population — depending on the size of the middle class in that country — gets an occasional glimpse of this heaven littered with consumer durables. Too bad if the rest are deprived of food, water, electricity and self-respect. Too bad if Kalahandi starves. This gang, consisting of finance ministers, World Bank and globalisation types, believes in its mission. Even though the gang members make massive profits — the bank makes money when it wants to eradicate poverty, finance ministers get votes by promising nirvana and globalisation pundits go on international talking and speaking circuits and collect frequent flyer miles in addition to hefty cheques — they act in the name of higher values.

Since religion cannot, by common definition, be validated or junked (how do you prove there's heaven, for heaven's sake), you either believe or you reject. True believers, genuinely pure of heart, exist in every religion and every finance ministry, but the majority just go along out of habit or helplessness. Development theories and globalisation models cannot be validated because no one has a complete and universally acceptable definition of what development means beyond GNP figures. For some, especially those politicians holding India's purse strings, it means the number of refrigerators consumed by the market or the number of multinationals present in the country. Too bad if these are disasters for the country and too bad if international lending institutions tie the amount of money they will give you as a loan to the number of multinationals you will allow into your country. This is what they call globalisation. This is what they term poverty reduction intervention. The World Bank has recently admitted that it has been increasingly including conditionalities to decide where it will put its money. The UN says nearly 100 developing countries that followed the bank's *mantras* and were hemmed in by its conditionalities have lower levels of income compared to the last decade.

Our leaders insist, like the institutions from which they borrow money, that an exclusively market-oriented model with a focus on poverty is not a contradiction in terms and will work if this "adjustment" can be managed. International lending institutions affirm that their policies are correct and the problem lies with those who have been asked to "adjust" because they have not applied the proper remedies hard enough or long enough. Not enough eggs have been broken.

In 1991, New Delhi embarked on a course of liberal economic reform that was to pave the way for India to become a global player, generate more wealth and create more jobs. The world sat up at the prospect of a 920-million-strong potential market and Wall Street types came up with every conceivable consumption pattern to prove India was worth exploring. In 1994, India signed the Uruguay Round multilateral trade pact without criticism, saying more eggs had to be broken if we wanted to eat omelettes.

In 1995, in a severe indictment of the government's economic policies, the Planning Commission of India revealed that poverty levels in the country had not declined significantly and jobs were not being created at the expected rate. It suggested that if all Indians had to remain on the same globe, the government would have to get serious about anti-poverty programmes and special rural works programmes.

Some figures presented in the Planning Commission's mid-term review of the eighth plan are vitally important. Poor people in the country — between 200 and 300 million — are eating less today than they did ten years ago. The availability of food per person had gone up from 395 grams per day to 525 grams per day between 1951 and 1991. However, despite robust growth in agricultural production, food availability levels had shrunk. Agricultural production reached 186 million tonnes in 1994-95. Yet, per capita food availability in the country plummeted. It was 468 grams per day in 1992, 464 grams in 1993 and 474 grams in 1994. In 1951, the per person availability of pulses was 61 grams per day and by 1958 this had gone up to 75 grams per day. This figure too plunged to 42 grams per day in 1991 and by 1994 it had shrunk to just 38 grams per day.

Prices in the country's public distribution system — through which people buy their rations — have gone up by 70-85 per cent during 1992-96. Agricultural labour's food bills are 80 per cent of their meagre incomes and the number of poor people before and after liberalisation has remained constant if not growing.

On 30 January 1996 the International Monetary Fund praised India's ambitious economic reforms but said much more needed to be done to rival the East Asian tigers in spurring growth and alleviating poverty. A 74-page report from Washington identified a long list of hurdles that finance policy makers were required to clear before India could truly globalise. The IMF singled out the need to narrow the budget deficit, improve infrastructure, curtail subsidies to loss-making firms, ease labour regulations and free agricultural trade. The government responded by stating that reforms would move forward gradually because of their unpopularity with certain categories of voters (remember the barbaric poor) and the need to rally support before pushing for change. The IMF also pointed out that India's long-term growth record had been disappointing, with per capita income increasing by less than 2 per cent a year since 1960 as compared with 5 to 6 per cent for the tigers and cubs of East Asia. Too few eggs...

How many eggs have to be broken before all Indians can eat? How many Indians would have died by the time an adequate number of eggs, acceptable to the globe, would have been broken?

PS: The World Bank has failed the world, just like the UN has, and there is little that nations like India can do to alter that. But when our elected representatives fail us, we have the right, at the very least, to ask some questions.

8 / GONGOS

In the beginning there were non-governmental organisations (NGOs). Operating outside the official realm, these groups defended anything from the environment to human rights to nuclear disarmament to baby seals and kept a constant watch over governments and exerted pressure on their elected representatives to deliver on their electoral promises. Over the years, NGOs have rendered great service to communities and nations, and even though every now and then they let their hearts bleed in public, there is no denying the fact that NGOs have served to make international trade and social relations more human and more bearable and governments more accountable. The United Nations takes them very seriously as do all international organisations. And while their methods, sometimes militant, have been questioned, the substance of their work is rarely in dispute.

That the NGO movement has made its mark is obvious from the various attempts governments — all governments — make to either buy them off, co-opt them or simply discredit their work and efforts. The accusation made most often against successful NGOs is that they accept funds from questionable sources and lobbies. While some of that is true, that fact is equally well known and that serves as a guard not just for the NGOs but also for people who value their work. And, in any case, it is not difficult to tell chalk from cheese in a world where information is available at your fingertips.

Then one fine day, Western governments got an idea. They decided to infiltrate the NGO movements in the developing countries to get a mudside view of how the poor lived, died and were arbitrarily detained in prisons by dictators. The Government of India hit on a better idea. It itself became an NGO, donned a wig and a moustache and let itself loose on the world stage. The GONGO — government non-governmental organisation — was born.

The Indian Government now has a policy to send a GONGO to every international meeting whether it be in Geneva, New York, Singapore or Sao Paulo. The role of the Indian GONGO is to keep one eye on Pakistan and the other on other enemies of India which may include journalists, judges and genuine Indian NGOs. So obvious is this network that often Indian officials can be seen handing out bits of paper and instructions to their GONGO in full view of the world. "Must we behave like this?" an Indian Supreme Court judge once remarked in Geneva when he saw a GONGO carrying a minister's bag. He was promptly labelled anti-national and immediately struck off from the official patronage list.

Every year, crores of rupees are spent on the Gongoisation of India. Hundreds of people with multicoloured wigs are sent to major international conferences ostensibly to defend India's interests through a complex web of lies and propaganda when even a child will tell you that the nation is better served when its people speak the truth. Hundreds and thousands of rupees are spent on identifying Western journalists, diplomats and negotiators who are "India-friendly" and these people are brought to the country at the national expense. A typical trip paid for by the Government of India will look something like this: Arrival in New Delhi, rest at five-star hotel, trip to Agra and Jaipur, return to Delhi to meet home and commerce ministry officials, Indian classical dance show in the evening, leave for Bangalore the next day and halt there for two days, followed by three days in Goa and one day in India's business centre Mumbai (alias Bombay) before flying out of the country. A slight variation is introduced if the Western intellectuals want to meet other intellectuals in New Delhi to exchange notes and addresses of good hotels all over the world. They are often accompanied by GONGOs whose job in India is to praise the foreign visitor till the guest turns blue in the face with embarrassment. A typical GONGO compliment is to praise the visitor's perspicacity when he says India will have to take care of its population problem before all else or that India cannot hope to globalise unless it first has proper roads that lead to its villages. The GONGO thinks he is subtle. During endless dinners and lunches while accompanying the foreign visitor (who, in most cases, is white and often male) he will slip in little bits and pieces of self-criticism and national breast-beating so that the visitor does not mistake India for Iraq or Saudi Arabia and goes back to report that Indians can actually criticise their leaders in public.

The GONGO will again touch base with the "foreigner" at an international conference in Geneva, New York or London and remind him about the trip to Jaipur. What he actually means is: "Remember there's no free lunch and if we paid for all those drinking sessions in Jaipur and Goa we expect you to hold India's hand when the world says we are killing people in our prisons.

We (GONGOs) expect you (white foreign intellectual) to stand up and say you were in India three months ago and even though roads are bad and there are too many people, most of them outside, on the streets, and not in the country's prisons."

The incest continues. The GONGO, in turn, gets invited abroad and this way Indians and foreigners travel back and forth at your expense defending your interests.

What do you have to do to become an Indian GONGO? It's easy — just ask one. You are actually quite lucky because I started out as a GONGO and now I head a GONGO recruiting agency in New Delhi. My office is just around the corner from South Block.

I am an Indian Government non-governmental organisation (GONGO). I am a rock. I am an island. I am a tree. I am a chemical. I am an amoeba. I am a low form of life. Now you see me, now you don't. Now you kick me, now you don't.

I have a fax, a modem, a computer and an electronic mail address. At a pinch, I can create my own web page on the Internet because I know some very intelligent people in American universities. I have no morals, no commitments, no self-respect and nobody, just nobody, can accuse me of being consistent. In fact, most of the time I don't know what I am talking about and sometimes I have even not been able to ascertain with any accuracy which meeting I am attending. But that has never posed a problem because my speeches are wailing sessions and are remote-controlled from New Delhi. Today I defend human rights in Geneva; tomorrow I am in Kashmir recycled as a lawyer; and the third day I lead a panel discussion at the India Multinational House in New Delhi where ministers and important officials clap after I speak and promise to pay me even better during my next trip abroad. In Geneva I curse Pakistan, in Kashmir I curse India and in New York I curse the weather. I also collect frequent flyer miles. These are very useful when my wife and children want to go shopping to Singapore. I wish the Government of India would pay for their shopping too, but then, I should not be too greedy, otherwise I will fall upon bad times. Contentment is the essence of life.

I must tell you that I have no brain. The government's desire is my command. The government's enemy is my enemy. The government's friend is my lord and master. If my government has one hole in the brain, I have two. I can be secular, muscular and avuncular as the occasion demands and, I am a quick-change artist who can shame the world's greatest actors. I only need seven minutes' advance notice to change my wig and shoes. Shoes are very important. They can give you away, depending on whether you are *chappal*-clad or Ferragamo- or Gucci-clad — you see, it makes all the difference. A man with a white shoe is an entire message. GONGOs have to keep these details in mind because we operate among important people who look at each other's shoes all day and all year long.

I have a wardrobe to suit every occasion. I can match dress to cause. I can look ethnic, modern, dirty (*jholawala* look), and I have masks that show anger, pain, rape and beating marks. In fact, New Delhi has promised to send me to Hollywood to learn the art of make-up from the team that made *ET, Jurassic Park*, etc. We have to prepare for the future, you know, especially at a time when India is globalising. I have stolen an NGO fashion catalogue from an American GONGO according to which pony tails are no longer fashionable for men.

I was also taught how to fax, e-mail and write to important politicians and American senators and British MPs from Kashmir or Kanyakumari. But in recent years, I have noticed that it is equally important to write to Indian intellectuals or, better still, invite them to seminars and panel discussions with fancy names like "Whither Kashmir?", "Is CTBT an Indian ploy or a Western toy?", "How many people would have to drown before Narmada can be saved?" etc. If you ask me, you should ask these intellectuals to read papers at these meetings — all of them are writing all the time with the result that nobody reads them any more in real life. If you tell them the panel discussion will revolve around their paper, they may even agree to come for free. Normally, they charge a hefty fee.

I can destroy any discussion but I have to admit that I have a preference for doing the "human rights show" because this is where my wardrobe and histrionics are best displayed. Let me show you how I have learnt to write the scripts for various occasions and what my opening, closing and crashing lines are. Here's a list of some of my activities. Actually, I will tell you about three of my favourite GONGO roles. These are: human rights, disarmament and environment and I have listed them not in any order of priority — GONGOs have no priority other than that decided by the hand that feeds them.

The Human Rights GONGO

Human rights GONGOs are in great demand because, in my humble opinion, they are the ones who can be meaningfully meaningful. That is to say they can say a lot without saying anything, promise the sky without committing themselves to anything, you know, like an election speech by an Indian politician. But not everyone can apply to be a human rights GONGO. You have to have that certain deprived look about you that can turn to anger at a wink or a nod from an Indian official. It's a good idea to come from the Chotanagpur region in Bihar. Most Indians including those babus in the foreign ministry don't know where that is and, by the time they find out, you will be sitting on a plane heading for Geneva where all-important human rights debates are held. Actually, I like Geneva a lot. Not much work, good food, same song, same dance, same people every year at the United Nations Human Rights Commission (UNHRC). In fact, last time I metamorphosed as a human rights GONGO at the UNHRC, I simply changed the dates on my speech, raised the number of killed and raped in Kashmir by 7000 and 2000, respectively, and changed my shoes just for that authentic touch.

What are human rights GONGOs supposed to say? Before I tell you that, let me show you how to dress for a UNHRC debate. Rule one: never wear a suit and never wear a pyjama. You have to find something in between so that you have that something Western, something Eastern look. If you look too well and Western then money won't come and if you look like a beggar people won't trust you. I know it's difficult, striking that balance;

but then life's tough as a GONGO. If you ask me, I'd wear normal trousers and a *khadi* shirt so that your intellectual moorings are upfront, a jacket, preferably a quilted one, because it can get quite cold, and a good pair of shoes. Besides quilted jackets give the impression that you are wearing a bullet-proof vest and that makes people think you are important. If you wear glasses, try to get one that makes you look like Trotsky — I know, it's amazing how some things never go out of fashion.

Now, you're all set. What? Speech. Don't worry, you have been chosen for this job because you have no brain, so don't try to show off. And, in any case, the Indian Government would have written one for you. You only have to remember to cry loudly when it says "cry" in the margin and whenever you say "Pakistani terrorist" rise slightly from your chair so that the cameras can get to work. You have to deny that the Indian police is brutal, that people die in Indian prisons and things like that and if you forget your lines, just blame it all on Pakistan. Don't feel bad because Pakistani GONGOs also blame India for all their problems; so the score is even. In addition you have to discredit all Indian civil liberties organisations as American spies. Many of them come to Geneva. You have to try and destroy their credibility by shouting at them in the lounge. The best way to do this is to ask as loudly as you can: "Who is paying you?, Who is paying you?" That will embarrass them. These civil liberties-types often talk to the Pakistanis in Geneva claiming they want to establish relations. If you spot the two together, you can do your "who is paying you" number then and there. And you have to tell at least 12 people every day that India is a democracy, Pakistan is not; we are multiethnic, they are not; we have Sardars, but they have Zardaris.... This I find rather hard to do because all white people like all Chinese and Japanese people look alike, so I have the feeling I am repeating myself to the same person. But who cares?

So I was telling you that I like Geneva. That's because unlike New York, Sao Paolo and Harare (I have visited these cities 19, 12 and 3 times, respectively), it's easy work. The city is safe and clean and there is no dust. Years of GONGO work can make you allergic to dust. We don't have anything much to do except harass a short list of Western diplomats, run to the photocopying machine behind the conference room every now and then and tail Pakistanis, especially when they go to the toilet because it has been found that often all their transactions take place there. And the coffee in the lounge is very good, just like the South Indian filter variety. It's a bit expensive but the Government of India thinks of everything. It even asks the wives of Indian diplomats to make food for us. And the city is so small that every evening you are driven to dinner and brought back at a respectable hour so that you can learn the lines for the next day. I must tell you that in Geneva, even the weekends are taken care of. The Indian embassy makes sure we have a steady supply of Indian films and foreign liquor to keep mind and body happy. What more could a GONGO ask for? The only problem is weight. It's quite difficult to remain trim with all this food and wine around. But all hope is not lost. I saw another cousin from Chotanagpur working for the Norwegians under the name of an NGO called World Unity for Despised Peoples, and he was fatter than I. That's because Norway is richer than India. You cannot win all around.

The Disarmament GONGO

This is a different bomb game altogether. You not only have to know not just ABCD, but you also have to be good in PCM — physics, chemistry and maths. That narrows the option immediately to certain parts of India. The disarmament type, unlike the human rights type, is a very clever person and that puts a strain on us because we have to show we are clever without appearing to be clever. You know, wisdom has to fall out of our pockets and mouths carelessly, just like that, without anyone feeling threatened. It's a bit like playing tennis with the boss — fight and then know when to lose. If you don't give him a good fight he won't promote you and if you win he'll sack you. Now you see, how difficult things are for us.

But first things first. We have to get the place-sense and dress-sense right. A disarmament GONGO has to be either from New Delhi or Chennai (alias Madras) Bombay is too filmy and Calcutta is too filthy and even though the latter can give Chennai a run for that long whining sound with intellectual variations, there's a strong preference for the South Indian, who, in addition to being weaned on PCM, is, in most cases, also a very good stenographer. Delhi is actually a good place to begin looking for potential candidates and, if you want my advice, try the India Multinational Centre where all these wannabe GONGOs with latent stenographic talent lie.

How does a disarmament GONGO dress? Quite smartly actually and he also wears his degree from Harvard and MIT on his sleeve. It's generally a good idea to dress up rather than down because of the unspoken rule.

Unspoken rule? Well, it goes without saying that if you are talking about weapons-grade material and plutonium and high-energy physics with a *jhola* on your shoulder and *pan* in your mouth, you might get mistaken for a poet who has lost his way. But there's not much chance of that happening because in nine out of ten cases, the disarmament GONGOs have spent a sabbatical photocopying a lot of papers in some strategic defence institute in Scandinavia, the United States or the UK. So when they return they actually manage to look quite dandy complete with linen suits, nifty briefcases and foreign wives who wear ready-made *salwar kameez* sets in bright colours. You may also grow your hair in an unruly fashion if you want people to ask you if you are related to Albert Einstein though the disarmament GONGO of late have been oiling their hair and combing it neatly into a pony tail.

What does the disarmament GONGO do? This GONGO, a peace-loving creature, is drawn to the world-without-nukes idea like a fly to honey, but what he detests most is the way the West has twisted this "principled position" to suit its own interests. For 50 years India has been whining about the injustice in all this — a low, grating sound that many in the Western world think is an excuse for India to develop its own nuclear arms industry. He shuttles beween Geneva and New York when he is not photocopying in Helsinki or Oslo.

The disarmament GONGO knows the world is divided into two types: The haves — and these are the five nuclear weapons states the US, the UK, France, China and Russia — and the rest, including India, Pakistan and Israel who are the nuclear wannabes. The disarmament GONGO's principal function is to sound so knowledgeable that no one, including his bosses in India, understands him. That is part ploy, part complex, but you will be amazed how effective it can be when he makes the the world feel bad about having nuclear weapons and India feel lousy about not having them at all at the same time with facts and figures that would send any computer out of business. The most important thing for a disarmament GONGO to remember is this whole thing about a "principled stand". In *principle* nukes are bad: Western nuclear doctrines are weak in the *principles* they defend; in *principle* India is a democracy; in *principle* India cannot defend anything if there is no *principle* to defend. The disarmament GONGO stands *for* everything that the world is against and is *against* everything that the world *is for*, which means India alternately lands next to Iraq or the US at the nuclear table without trying very hard. Which, in short, explains India's principled position in matters such as these.

The Environment GONGO

The environment GONGO is generally a small woman with grey hair; from Madhya Pradesh or Gujarat, carrying *khadi* files from Gurjari. Don't ask why. That is how things are. Probably because the government has decided that since the environment issue attracts women in large numbers all over the world, what better ploy than to break that solidarity with the help of mainstream women? Clever. Clever.

The environment GONGO typically wears a saree, is kind and soft-spoken and walks fast as if running to save a falling tree. Don't wear silk sarees because silk is made from boiling worms and that is a very cruel thing to do. Cotton is the best. In addition to giving everyone around you a bad conscience, you indirectly promote Mahatma Gandhi. Colours have to be kind too: you know, whites and pastels. And no make-up. It's a good idea to wash your hair in *shikakai* (no synthetic smells, please) and allow it to dry in the wind and if someone asks you what that smell around you is, you can say it's the wind in the trees. There's another advantage to this natural look — at the end of the day you look as tired as your cause. You are also a vegetarian. It's better for the image. Once I was asked this stupid question by a stupid white who walked up to me in Geneva and wondered aloud: "Are you a vegetarian because you hate trees?" and implied that I ate trees because I didn't like them!! There's no limit to degeneration in the West. It's not a question of having a sense of humour. When you are a GONGO, you have no sense of humour.

The environment GONGO has her job cut out. She has to do two things. First and foremost she has to accuse that Narmada gang of being bought off by Western environmentalist lobbies which don't want India to progress and, secondly, she has to quote chapter and verse from our scriptures to show that we in India hugged trees and prayed to them at a time when the Western world was full of shrubs. The environment GONGO has to deny that India buys toxic waste from the West and if you find that you are losing that argument (between you and me, we do booming business in this) just turn around, flick your hair and ask authoritatively why the West produces so much waste in the first place. That will stump them all.

You will be working a lot in Geneva where the environment is very good. The important thing is to ensure that you don't bump into any other GONGO (human rights, disarmament) with whom you trained at my behind-the-South Block office in New Delhi.

Now that I have told you everything about how Gongos work, let me share a problem with you. I have heard that the government is angry with me. The same government that took me out of my original surroundings — grassroots — and transplanted me in international fora now says it is terrified of my act. In the beginning, I was trained to cry when the lights came on, shout when the taperecorder was switched on and limp when approached by a white diplomat. I practised hard and by the time I was let loose, I could do all that and fall off my chair at the same time.

Part of my original job was also to spot imposters and inform governments when their inner circles were being infiltrated by the scum of the earth. Now even my bosses don't want to see me. They say I am an embarrassment, I shout too much, my wig is always showing, my saree makes me look like a beggar and that I have become fat. Some nasty people have now made it their business to inform other people about me and warn them that human rights debates have been turned into torture chambers by me and my friends. In fact, my mentors in New Delhi are saying very nasty things about Pakistani and American GONGOs in my presence. I wonder what they really say about me behind my back. You know, they make me criticise the World Bank in Geneva and then they go to the same bank in Washington begging for money.

I am baffled. Governments created me. I am defending their cause. Now they want to destroy me. I feel like the mad cow.

9

NTPC, XYKZ, CTBT
or National Defence

In August 1996, India told the world it would not accept a nuclear test ban treaty that did not address its national security interests and blocked a major international effort to force New Delhi into accepting such a treaty. The world told New Delhi it would face international criticism. New Delhi replied if that was the price to pay for self-respect, then so be it. The world said India was being anti-West. India replied that it was not a question of being anti-West or anti anything else for that matter but pro-Indian. New Delhi went on to say in its view the two were not incompatible, a position that few understood or had the courage to understand.

The first call for a ban on nuclear tests was made by Prime Minister Jawaharlal Nehru who, in 1954, said the time had come for a "standstill agreement to halt all testing of nuclear weapons" with a view to ridding the world of what India perceived as a deadly weapon of mass destruction. A test ban was a necessary first step, but in no way the ultimate step which could only be one that rids the world of nuclear weapons. A success of sorts was achieved when the world got the partial test ban treaty (PTBT, 1963) which banned atmospheric tests. This treaty was hailed by some as a milestone and questioned by others who felt that all PTBT did was drive testing away from the atmosphere to under the ground. Countries that questioned the use of half measures wanted the world to sign a "comprehensive" test ban treaty that would pave the way for complete nuclear disarmament.

A comprehensive test ban treaty (CTBT) has been one of the most sought-after and equally elusive arms control measures. Actual negotiations for a test ban that would prohibit all nuclear explosions, including underground explosions, have been taking place periodically since 1958 both in a limited East-West context and in the broader multilateral forums but it was only in 1994 that serious negotiations got underway. For 18 months, countries negotiating the draft text of the treaty in Geneva could not reach any consensus on what the treaty was supposed to ban and what it would allow, who would have to sign it for the treaty to enter into force and, most importantly, would the world be a safer place once the CTBT was in the bag?

There was a vigorous domestic debate in India about what the treaty meant for a country flanked on one side by a nuclear weapons state and on the other by a nuclear wannabe which had clandestine arms transfers from the nuclear weapons state. It was clear from the start that the CTBT negotiations (a mandate for which was co-sponsored by India at the UN in New York) had been hijacked by the US, UK, China, Russia and France, the five nuclear weapons states, to suit an international agenda that had little to do with dismantling the nuclear weapons industry. What made matters worse was that India was being forced to accept a treaty that completely ignored its regional reality. It also became painfully evident during the often acrimonious negotiations in Geneva that the P5 (thus called because they are the five permanent members of the UN Security Council) held together because they were suspicious of one another and each wanted to keep the other in check. They brought this equation to the CTBT talks and tried to spread it across the board, fanning new fears (e.g., press reports that India had conducted a second nuclear explosion) that disappeared upon examination.

In January 1996, India said at the negotiations that the indefinite extension of the nuclear non-proliferation treaty (NPT) in 1995 — a gift the nuclear weapons states have bestowed upon themselves and one which gives them and them only the right to blow the world apart — was an act of bad faith. Given that reality, it was imperative to link a CTBT to a specific time-bound procedure for carrying out disarmament. More importantly, India said if a CTBT was to be meaningful it "...should be securely anchored in the global disarmament context and be linked through treaty language to the elimination of all nuclear weapons in a time-bound framework...so that the CTBT does not just become a flawed instrument aimed at curbing horizontal proliferation but a genuine disarmament step". India drew attention to the PTBT and clarified that just like that flawed treaty had driven testing underground, it would be a shame if the CTBT drove testing into laboratories. That is precisely what has happened. The world has a CTBT, but no commitment from anyone about the elimination of nuclear weapons. Instead, billions of dollars are heading for laboratories from where a fourth generation of weapons will continue to maintain the balance of terror.

Was there pressure on India to accept the international regime? Is the Pope Catholic?

The rest of the world, used to India posturing before caving in, made the mistake of interpreting India's security concern too as a pre-electoral posture. India will fall in line after the general elections in May 1996, negotiators in Geneva thought.

What did India do? Nothing much. It simply stood up up like an adult and told the rest of the world, in this case, the P5 that they would have to go ahead with their version of the CTBT without New Delhi. There was no call for Third World solidarity, Non-Aligned this and Group of 77 that. There was no long whining sound, no drama. Just the logic of a clear-headed adult who could walk alone.

What are you thinking? If we can do it once…

The bank clerk looked at the name and then up at her. He checked the name again, leaned over the desk and asked the lady: "You are doing NTPC in Geneva, aren't you?"

She smiled, but before she could answer, the clerk said: "Don't move. The entire nation is behind you. Just don't move. Don't give in — okay?"

The chief Indian negotiator was surprised. Her heart pinched a little. The clerk had got something wrong and something right. She was negotiating the comprehensive test ban treaty (CTBT) for India in Geneva, not the NTPC or the CBDT, as it had been once called, or the XYKZ. But the clerk's remarks showed that the penny had dropped. He couldn't tell CTBT from the other letters in the alphabet, but beyond the detail and the drama in Geneva, New Delhi and New York, he had understood that the talks concerned India's security and this item on the national agenda was non-negotiable. Some things are logical and simple. You don't have to be a genius to understand that. You don't require an "intellectual" to interpret that.

The funny thing about the CTBT is that those who didn't want the treaty were saying the same things about it as those like India who wanted it. The nuclear weapons states — the United States, the UK, France, Russia and China which are also the five permanent members of the United Nations Security Council — held the view that the test ban treaty was an indispensable step towards nuclear disarmament. It would be good for global health, global environment, and global safety that the treaty be in place before September 1996 and they invited parts of the globe away from theirs to start falling in line. But when India wanted the nuclear weapons states to lead the way to such global enlightenment, the five baulked, refused to translate words into deeds in the form of a time-bound commitment to eliminate nuclear weapons and called India a treaty-spoiler. In the ultimate analysis, they said, India was right about asking nuclear weapons to be wiped out from the face of this earth but could New Delhi please look at a "in-the-meantime" framework. India replied it had been waiting on the "in-the-meantime" fence since 1954 and that was a lot of years and a lot patience.

Look at it logically. Among themselves, the five nuclear weapon powers have conducted some 2000 explosions, while denying that right to every other country in the world through a series of discriminatory treaties including the nuclear non-proliferation treaty (NPT). Today, the nuclear debate concerns eight countries. Namely, P5 and India, Pakistan and Israel, the three threshold states which are believed to have the capability to put a few bombs together within 24 hours.

It's not a question of whether nuclear weapons are good or bad. There is possibly nobody in this world who will say that nuclear weapons are good. But a lot of people will affirm that they are a reality and a very frightening one at that. The negotiations in Geneva were about what is good and what is real with the latter, as usual, carrying the day. The CTBT was aimed primarily at the three threshold states — India, Pakistan and Israel. The last, we all know, "allows" Washington to be the boss in the region while it pulls the strings in America. Pakistan has one eye riveted on the US and the other on China and has made it plain it will sign the CTBT only if India does. What does that leave?

The CTBT was to be a qualitative cap, a measure to freeze the nuclear status quo in today's terms so that those who have nuclear weapons continue to have them and improve their quality till kingdom come and those who don't remain without them till hell freezes over. Some things are indeed very simple. In CTBT everybody's logic was also intact.

Let's start at the very beginning, at the UN General Assembly in 1993 which gave the then 38-nation Geneva-based CD (Conference on Disarmament) its first full-fledged mandate to negotiate a comprehensive test ban treaty as soon as possible. The scope of the treaty soon emerged as the most important and most contentious aspect of the negotiations. What were the countries to ban? Linked to the scope of the treaty was the equally important issue of verification and, to that, compliance with the treaty's obligations and a series of inspection measures that would identify possible cheaters and determine the extent to which they had strayed from their commitments. There was to be an international monitoring system that would detect cheaters, but it was unclear what techniques would be used by this system to find out who was cheating. In addition, there was another twist to the on-site inspection issue. What was the process that would trigger an on-site inspection? There were genuine fears that this inspection would be turned into a fishing expedition to which a group of powerful countries would use information non-transparently gathered to find out what other countries were doing in their nuclear facilities. The US wanted to use its own technical "expertise" to detect cheaters in addition to those set up by the treaty. Many countries, including China, felt this was an euphemism for shooting off spy satellites and that monitoring by the treaty's own architecture (over 50 monitoring stations spread all over the world) was all that should be allowed. As the endgame came into focus, the scope of the treaty blurred and with it every other aspect of the test ban treaty. There was such a rush to finish everything even before negotiators could agree on what they were trying to do, that, at one point in the negotiations, many diplomats started looking out of the window wondering if the draft treaty text would land on the table from heaven.

There was no official deadline, but the keepers of this world decided that it would look rather cute if the president of the United States had a CTBT in his pocket to pull out and wave to crowds when he got into an electoral mode in 1996. So, working backwards from the US election campaign, the world concluded that a CTBT should be ready by August 1996 at the very latest which would give translators and lawyers six weeks to have a shiny new CTBT on the table when the UN met for its annual session in New York in October.

To be fair, the only country that would have won all around — with or without the treaty — was the United States, so advanced with its nuclear technology that there's little hope (and even lesser money) that the other P4 will ever catch up. But a CTBT would freeze America's superiority and others' lack of it and who doesn't like to be the boss? The UK with no site of its own is totally dependent on the US for this activity and, as some negotiators joked during the test ban treaty talks, the UK is "nuclearly" attached to America. The US and the UK are linked through a series of nuclear information exchange programmes that ensures Washington's supremacy. As a consequence, it was subservient to the US position during the CTBT talks, a position that must have led to a lot of anger and frustration that was evident during the talks, especially when Great Britain was told off by a former colony called India.

France. Look at what this country said in the late 1950s. At a press conference on 23 October 1958, General Charles de Gaulle, who set France on the nuclear armaments course, declared: "We will continue to press the Russians, the Americans and the British to agree to halt production of nuclear weapons, liquidate their stocks and agree to an effective international control. If this goal were attained, the famous question of nuclear tests would immediately disappear. If this were not to be, to those who continue to accumulate bombs, how would a suspension of tests make any difference? Their power would not be diminished. It would be on the contrary a hoax on the poor world, if these three states make the world believe that by suspending tests we would be enhancing world security. It would even be giving themselves an alibi for not disarming.... France, at a time when the other three (the USA, the USSR and the UK) remain overarmed, cannot agree to a gigantic and chronic inferiority."

Sounds like India, doesn't it? In fact, this is exactly what India said at the CTBT negotiations 36 years after Charles de Gaulle had spoken. When the Indian negotiator stuck this statement under her French counterpart's nose, the reply was a snub and a sneer. France, opposed to test bans, felt that if a country is not "nuclearly" credible, it is not credible at all. It has argued that it needs tests to stay up to date with military technology and that nuclear weapons are crucial to France's status as a global power. France's position has always been a muddled one, driven a lot by its very French desire to be different. It has always felt the need to modernise its weapons as a "deterrent" but has deep-rooted and genuine fears that French advances in nuclear weapons technology have been overtaken by at least one if not two generations of weapons by its superpower rivals. It decided to join the CTBT, analysts say, because it felt the treaty would hold the weapons curve constant and even though that meant playing second fiddle to the US and by extension the UK; that was better than being overtaken by others. The French conducted nuclear tests during the CTBT negotiations and then joined an international moratorium and signed a deal with the US that gave it access to computer-simulated data hitherto reserved only for the UK. It had entered the hallowed circle of the "Brahmins" among the P5. The CTBT negotiations showed this caste system up very blatantly. The US, the UK and France negotiated as one. China was alone and Russia, on a respirator for some years now, pulled in all directions and criticised India because it could not openly criticise the US.

Russia came through very badly during the negotiations, indicating that even though outwardly its leaders were holding on to America's and, more accurately, to the World Bank's hands, there was strong resentment in the country about being kicked around by its most famous former enemy. In fact, there was strong resistance from the country's military establishment to accepting a treaty that would place the country, once a superpower, permanently on its knees in front of the US. Russia had a large programme for peaceful nuclear explosions (PNEs) and giving them up, as the CTBT required, would severely restrict them. As the talks progressed — or regressed, to be more accurate — sections of the ruling elite got more vocal about their opposition to the treaty. They pointed to the eastward expansion of the NATO and argued that if Russia gave up its only-perfected nuclear testing option, it would stand almost naked against the advance of the US and its allies into its backyard. But, the Russian president, with a world-famous weakness for alcohol, was too busy pleasing the US to listen, with the result that the Russian negotiators vent their ire on India, which was a former Soviet ally that had stood up to the rest of the world.

China did its "Hindi-Chini Bhai Bhai" act till it became clear as daylight that Beijing, along with Russia, did not want a treaty that would ensure that the two remain below the P3 and looked around for a scapegoat to hang a dead treaty on. China said it wanted the treaty to allow PNEs because it had dams and roads to build and criticised the US for wanting to use spy satellites to detect cheaters. In fact, the balance of suspicion became even more obvious when China and the US wanted monitoring stations to be set up at each other's testing sites! Beijing made a lot of noise during the talks, leading diplomats to wonder if this public, anti-US posture at the test ban talks was aimed at securing concessions in other areas, namely, trade. As it turned out, China went along with the P3 and pushed for a CTBT that only banned explosions.

The negotiations to rid the world of nuclear weapons came at a time when the government in India was extremely fragile and was not in a position to make any foreign policy move that could bring it down before the elections. Most people in India, like the bank clerk, didn't really know what CTBT was all about — they had other immediate problems — except that it concerned nuclear bombs, Pakistan, the United States and China. But there was some residual interest in disarmament issues and the residue boiled over every now and then when it seemed that India was being pushed against the wall. Some lobbies in the country turned the negotiations into a free for all anti-American match. Others, especially "intellectuals" remote-controlled from Iceland and Finland, lectured to the nation about the need to hold America's hand. The government, trying to walk between these two extreme positions, found itself domestically and internationally vulnerable. Signing the CTBT would be political death. Not signing it would mean setting itself up for international censure and possible abuse by three-letter words like IMF. You would have thought New Delhi would do what it does best — moralise, wail, and then cave in, blaming "them" for isolating it.

Wake up and smell the roses. India didn't do that. In fact, when the entire world asked the chief Indian negotiator in Geneva if her country was not afraid of being isolated, she shot back: "How do you isolate 900 million people?" Makes you feel good, doesn't it? A little bit of self-respect every now and then is such a nice thing!

Take it, or leave it — somewhere it all came through together. At home and abroad. The message that had got through to Bangalore, Ranchi, Vijayawada and Cuttack was that India's security interests were being taken care of in an intelligent manner. Abroad, it became evident, as days passed, that elections or no elections, minority government or majority government, the country's mind was made up as far as the CTBT was concerned. It didn't matter if the Indian position was anti-American or anti-Russian or anti-anything for that matter. Equally inconsequential was the fact that India, among the first countries in the world to call for a halt to nuclear tests, was now backing off from the draft of a text that would give the world some kind of a test ban treaty. India's unwillingness to sign the CTBT after co-sponsoring its negotiating mandate was variously interpreted. There were those who said New Delhi had changed its mind because it had a secret nuclear weapons programme; there were others who said India was never serious about a CTBT; and there were yet others who said the country has no nuclear policy worth its name and the attitude to the CTBT was a knee-jerk reaction to Western pressure. What is fair to say is that New Delhi has not had a coherent national debate on nuclear issues, including nuclear weapons issues, and our politicians are fairly clueless about how they plan, in the long run, to cope with an aggressive nuclear weapons power and neighbour called China. However, in the context of the CTBT, these observations seemed irrelevant because India's nuclear option or lack of it had to be the result of a home-grown debate and not the product of international pressure. It was an internal matter. This was the position in Geneva. The readout in London, Washington, Beijing and Moscow was that putting India in a position where it would have to choose between internal pressure and external pressure was a bad place to start and finish. Unfortunately, the keepers of the world's nuclear conscience, but more so China and Russia, insisted that if India did not sign on the dotted line, there was little point in having a CTBT. It's a bit like telling you I will build a wall around your house and you have no right to complain. Simple and, this time around, ridiculously short-sighted.

Pushed to the brink, India grew. Like all responsible adults it defended its interests and principles with an equanimity reserved for mature nations and which we in India have few and fleeting glimpses of. Nothing mattered any more. There was none of that long whining sound. This was a nation telling the world where it got off. It didn't matter if governments in India changed at a critical juncture in the negotiations; it didn't matter if the world's major powers had stepped up bilateral and multilateral pressure on India; and it didn't matter if India, in the words of some Indians, was "isolated". There was a national consensus on CTBT — it said the country's security was non-negotiable. Even the bank clerk grasped that. There was no whining sound in Geneva.

Now, wait a minute. How is it that in other areas critical to India's long-term security — infrastructure, self-sufficiency in food, environment and telecom — there's no common sense and no national consensus? Keep asking, and while you are at it you might also ask yourself why we go into a tailspin wondering what "they" — the United States, Russia, Saturn and the neighbours — will say if we defend our interests? Why does pro-Indian automatically mean anti-something else? Makes you wonder, doesn't it?

Anyway, throughout the 18 months that the test ban negotiations lasted, India did not lose track of its self. It is fleeting moments like these that show us that not all our politicians and bureaucrats are thinking with their feet, and, when push comes to shove, we don't blame American culture, Boris Yeltsin and the weather in London for India's problems. But, there's a flip side to this and the flip side hurts. When you know that you have what it takes to reach for the stars but have to settle for the ditch because some illiterate equation has to be accommodated, it hurts so badly that you cannot help asking yourself who decides for India.

But the world didn't know that you see. The world didn't know what? Well, you see, ever since the country has liberalised and decided to go global, which means other parts of the globe have discovered India, the only thing they have been hearing is that long whining sound. You know, the roads are full of holes because the municipal corporation and the civil engineer cheat. They cheat because the government cheats. The government cheats because it is full of people who feel cheated by the British, *kismat* and their neighbours. The world had got so used to this long whining sound during the last five years that when India told the test ban negotiators they could go and jump into the nearest lake and take their treaty with them, many interpreted it as pre-Indian election bravado that would soon be replaced by...you said it!

So, throughout the talks two questions doing the rounds in Geneva were: "How many phone calls can the Indian prime minister take" and "what will the prime minister say when the president of the United States rings him a second time?" It is not known if those calls were made. Maybe the prime minister was sleeping when the phone rang or another possibility could be that the two men failed to understand each other — it's a long way from Little Rock to Haradhanahalli. But no external pressure worked.

There was another spin on the sin. Indian negotiators in Geneva had to cope not just with fire from their adversaries, but also from what has come to be known as "friendly fire". You know, those interest groups in India remote-controlled from Iceland, or Indian intellectuals who always talk about political realities when the rest of the world is talking about national security and vice versa. As the CTBT war raged, there were fears of friendly fire and sabotage coming not from Washington, London or Beijing but from New Delhi. That didn't wash either and it took just a handful of people — three negotiators in Geneva and three in New Delhi formed the core — to keep the country's self-respect together.

So, we were saying that nobody wanted the CTBT. Now that the world's nuclear conscience keepers have their full-of-holes treaty, let's bet that weapons' laboratories all over the world are going to be busier than during the Cold War. You would be a fool if you think that, post-CTBT, thousands of nuclear scientists cheerfully cleaned their desks and packed their bags and prepared to go fishing for the rest of their lives. There is every indication that the opposite is happening and the CTBT, like its cousin the NPT, is a farce.

India refused to sign the treaty for two basic reasons. First, it said the CTBT was *not* a comprehensive ban on nuclear testing as all it did was replace one technology with another. Okay, it banned explosions, but allowed sophisticated laboratory testing (subcritical tests) to continue and while the West claimed that these tests were necessary to keep their weapons "ready", India asked ready for what, since the stated aim was to rid the world of such "readiness" and allied nervousness. Let's face it. As nuclear science develops, new weapons technologies will emerge that cannot be foreseen or restricted. Fourth generation nuclear weapons based on atomic or nuclear processes (without nuclear explosions) will not be restricted by the CTBT. In contrast to the second generation nuclear weapons (broadly stated, the first generation weapons are all uranium or all plutonium based, the second generation are two-stage thermonuclear devices, the third generation nuclear weapons are "tailored" or "enhanced" special effects warheads), their development is essentially science based making use of recent advances in fundamental or applied research. In common with the first generation they allow for rather simple or rugged designs, although the special materials they will be made of might be much more difficult to manufacture than plutonium or enriched uranium. Fourth generation nuclear weapons are slated to provide really significant military advantages since most of them will produce no residual radioactivity. But the biggest advantage will be political since their development will be restricted to the most technologically advanced countries such as the United States. So, when India said ban lab tests, the world said ban India. Secondly, India wanted the P5 to commit themselves to a time-bound framework within which they would destroy their nuclear weapons as they have been telling us since the dawn of the nuclear day that their eventual goal is to make the world nuclear weapons free. Intelligent, no? And so very logical, you'd say. Indeed. The logic was on India's side. The world had failed its CTBT mandate.

The United Nations mandated the Conference on Disarmament (CD) "to negotiate intensively a universal and multilaterally effective and verifiable comprehensive nuclear test ban treaty, which would contribute effectively to the prevention of the proliferation of the nuclear weapons in all its aspects, to the process of nuclear disarmament and therefore to the enhancement of international peace and security". In other words, the CD — the world's only multilateral forum for negotiating disarmament matters — was to negotiate a "comprehensive" treaty and not one that simply banned nuclear blasts including undergound ones. This was not an environment-related treaty wherein the release of nuclear energy would kill the birds and fish. This was a serious matter, India said. France responded by announcing a series of blasts in the South Pacific Ocean; the United States asserted it had planned a series of subcritical tests for late 1996 and early 1997; and China timed its nuclear tests precisely with the opening of each CD session.

India insisted that the scope of the CTBT was skewed. The text on the table — which the UN said should be a negotiated one but which, in reality, just fell from the sky one day — left too many loopholes that would permit nuclear weapons states to continue refining and developing their nuclear arsenals at their test sites and laboratories. The CTBT, New Delhi pointed out, should be placed in its proper disarmament context, as part of a step-by-step process aimed at achieving the complete elimination of *all* nuclear weapons within a time-bound framework. In the recent past, the NPT had been extended indefinitely. This single act resulted in the legitimisation, for the foreseeable future and beyond, of the possession by a few states and their possible use as a currency of power. Countries around India (China and Pakistan), New Delhi reminded the rest of the world, continued their weapons programmes openly or clandestinely. "We would not accept any language in the treaty text which would affect our sovereign right to decide, in the light of our supreme national interest, whether we should or should not accede to the treaty," the chief Indian negotiator told an increasingly nervous CD.

Don't be a pain, the West admonished, adding that the "public" wanted the CTBT. Which public? India's chief negotiator asked, and wondered at a public discussion whether the country's 900 million people were also part of this "public" or not. "We cannot accept that it is legitimate for some countries to rely on nuclear weapons for their security while denying this right to others," India affirmed. The logic was intact. And it was simple even for the residents of Haradhanahalli, who by this time had taken over New Delhi, to understand.

India's assessment of the P5's nuclear agenda was borne out by related developments preceding and during the negotiations. The Cold War doctrines were being replaced by a whole new set of calculations, on the basis of which specific countries and regions were being targeted. A new doctrine had been developed that nuclear weapons were required as a precaution against the future errant behaviour and threat from unspecified states east of Turkey and west of Tokyo — get it? Nuclear testing was being carried out even as countries in Geneva promised to stop them. Three of the P5 — the US, the UK and France — declared that laboratory tests were important for them to complete work on new designs and gather data to enable computer simulation and modelling to define and refine future prototypes of weapons. When it became clear to New Delhi that it was talking to the wall, it blocked the treaty, proclaiming: "This is not the CTBT India envisaged in 1954. This cannot be the CTBT that India can be expected to accept." Feels goods, doesn't it?

Was India being a pain? Hardly, but then that viewpoint depends on whose hurt you think is more important than yours.

Contrary to expectations that a CTBT would halt nuclear weapons development and lead inexorably to disarmament, nuclear research development and testing continue (and will do so) unabated. In the United States, for example, the National Ignition Facility (NIF) planned for the Lawrence Livermore National Laboratory is intended to produce miniature thermonuclear explosions to provide data for the "advance" of nuclear weapons science. Slated to go on-line in 2002, ten years after the Cold War has ended and peace has broken out like smallpox all over the world, the NIF represents the single largest military programme ever planned for the Livermore Lab. It will cost more than $1 billion to build, with a projected lifetime cost of over $4.5 billion, and is considered as the most expensive element of a vast laboratory-based infrastructure to preserve the capacity to maintain, test, modify, design and produce nuclear weapons well into the next century with or without underground testing. Analysts explain that we are looking at 200 lasers that can focus on heavy hydrogen to produce the sort of temperatures you would find in a fusion bomb. The US Department of Energy's (DOE's) multibillion dollar "stockpile stewardship and management (SS&M)" programme includes an elaborate system of high-tech laboratory facilities consisting of explosives-testing installations as large as sports stadiums, extensive new manufacturing capabilities and the world's fastest supercomputers. All this money would be spent in addition to the estimated $4 trillion that the world's strongest country had spent on nuclear weapons over the last 50 years. In October 1995, the DOE announced that it planned to conduct two "subcritical high-explosive experiments with nuclear materials" underground at the Nevada test site in 1996 and four subcritical experiments in 1997.

Now why would anyone do all this if they are preparing to rid the world of nuclear weapons? Doesn't make sense, does it?

When the US president announced in 1995 that he wanted a "zero yield" (no explosions) CTBT, he endorsed, in the same breath, the SS&M programme as a necessary means of maintaining the US nuclear deterrent without underground testing. In addition, he said the United States would re-examine all its international commitments, including those required by the CTBT, if these ran counter to America's "supreme national interest".

What are subcritical tests and why is it an issue with India?

Subcritical tests are those that use anything between 50 and 500 pounds of high-explosive charge and involve special nuclear materials including plutonium, but the experiments do not produce a self-sustaining chain reaction — hence subcritical. According to nuclear weapons scientists, these tests are needed to improve the dynamic properties of aged nuclear materials (i.e., plutonium) in order to first assess the effects of new manufacturing techniques on weapons' performance and, secondly, maintain the capabilities of the Nevada test site and support nuclear test "readiness". The two tests scheduled for 1996 — and which were reportedly postponed — would ostensibly provide the DOE with additional data on the behaviour of plutonium in a "strongly-shocked state" — data that is said to be needed for improving supercomputer modelling of nuclear weapon performance and assessing changes in weapon remanufacture techniques and materials. Each experiment would cost an estimated $20 million. Lot of money, isn't it, for an establishment that claims it wants to wind down and eliminate nuclear weapons.

The good news is that America is a democracy and while that might not mean the same thing to blacks in the deep south as it does to a white in Washington, the country has a healthy press with a strong tradition of leaks. And sooner or later things leak. So, while US negotiators screamed themselves blue in the face denying that there was anything wrong with subcritical tests, a pesky document from the DOE started circulating on Internet announcing the opposite. The document — downloaded immediately in Geneva — showed that the US DOE publicly acknowledged that its nuclear scientists were investigating "major changes" to existing nuclear warheads as well as "entirely new (weapons) designs". The document on the Worldwide Web blew the bottom out of the DOE's earlier claims that the nation's nuclear weapons' laboratories — Lawrence Livermore, Sandia and Los Alamos — were involved only in minor weapon modifications and the surveillance of existing arsenal and that most of the scientists were preparing to go fishing.

The DOE document surfaced just as the US administration unveiled a request to raise nuclear weapons spending by $228 million in 1997, out of which $191 million would go to the Lawrence Livermore Laboratory's NIF, the giant laser designed to simulate thermonuclear explosions. The document also conceded that the new weapons' studies were not necessarily being requested by the Department of Defence, the lab's traditional customer, suggesting that there were doughnuts within doughnuts in the administration. The document further divulged that concepts under consideration ranged in complexity from relatively minor modifications in the components of existing weapons to major changes in warhead subsystems to entirely new physics designs for a proposed or candidate weapon.

The French, for their part, are building a similar, though more modest, facility near Bordeaux — Project Megajoules — as part of an experimental programme expected to swallow $1.3 billion over the next five years. The Russians are working long and late hours at their Arctic test range in Novya Zemlya and while no one is able to pinpoint what they are doing, it is highy unlikely that they are building a snowman. Their interest in subcritical experiments indicates that the CTBT is a cover.

The Chinese argued in Geneva that they needed the CTBT to exclude the so-called "peaceful nuclear explosions" from the Geneva text because they wanted to dig a 500-mile irrigation canal through rough mountain terrain in Tibet.

As negotiations regressed it became clear that the P5 were preparing to replace brain with brawn. When the Geneva conference and the legitimate CD track failed, they decided to hijack the fractured text and take it directly to the UN in New York — as opposed to the CD forwarding it as an agreed text — and push it through in a wheelchair. It was opened for signature just in time for the US elections.

The world, believe it or not, didn't fall apart. India defended its interests. The P5 got their treaty. The world is not any more safe today than it was before the CTBT and that is why India refused to sign the text. It's amazing how simple things are when you know what you want. National interest, like national security, is national interest and national security by any other name. Even the bank clerk got that. All else is deliberate confusion, imagined fears and real complexes.

Index

Agricultural production, 168
America, United States of, 63, 98, 99, 100, 101, 106, 109, 112, 114, 118, 120, 125, 160, 195, 197, 201, 204, 209, 210, 211
   1929 crash in, 160
   depression in, 160
   Super 301 against India, 113, 117
   trade sanctions by, 99
Arafat, Yasser, 84, 93
Article 370, 47
"Azad Kashmir", 45

Babri Masjid, 29
   demolition of, 29
Bharatiya Janata Party (BJP), 29

Bhutto, Benazir, 85
Bureaucrats, i, 6, 89, 105, 106, 109, 204

Caste system, 10
Chakravarty Raghavan, 100
China, 17, 24, 45, 108, 159, 181, 197, 200, 201, 203, 208, 213
   and CTBT, 200-201, 203, 213
   and human rights, 24
Comprehensive Test Ban Treaty (CTBT), 105, 178, 191-213
   and China, 200-201
   and France, 198-99
   and India, 105, 191, 199, 202, 206, 209

and Russia, 200
and United Kingdom, 200
and USA, 196-98
debate in India on, 192
Conference on Disarmament, 196-97, 207
and China, 208
and France, 207
and India, 207
and USA, 208
Congress Party, 47

Davos, iii, 79, 80, 82-94
as a businessmen's club, 83
as international *bazar*, 79, 85
Developing countries, 97-102, 107, 110, 111, 113, 157, 159, 164, 167, 174
Disarmament, 182

Elections, 11
and politicians, 11
Environment, 184
European Union, 98, 108, 112, 125

Foreign Direct Investment (FDI), 158
for developing countries, 159

France, 195, 198, 207, 209, 213
and CTBT, 198-99
money spent on nuclear weapons, 213
nuclear tests by, 199, 209

Gandhi, Mahatma, 101, 145
Gaulle, General Charles de, 198
General Agreement on Tariffs and Trade (GATT), 12, 97, 99, 106, 117
Geneva, 10, 23, 25, 27, 30, 32, 57, 106, 180, 203, 205
Globalisation, 7, 13, 145-69
and India, 158-59
and liberalisation, 154-56
and prices, 157
gains of, 161

Human Rights, 23, 24, 27, 48, 49, 111, 173, 177, 178
as a weapon against developing countries, 24

India, 3, 4, 5, 6, 7, 8, 9, 12, 24, 27, 33
agricultural production in, 168

India.....contd.

    and Uruguay Round negotiations, 97-98, 102, 103, 104, 122, 123, 167
    and CTBT, 105, 191, 199, 202, 206, 209
    and globalisation, 158-59
    and human rights, 24
    and intellectual property rights negotiations, 112-13, 114, 115
    and World Bank, 150
    as a poor country, 10-11
    caste system in, 10
    confrontation with Pakistan, 28, 29, 45, 46
    corruption in, 16
    culture in, 90-91
    elections in, 11
    foreign direct investments in, 123-24
    investments in, 80, 86, 107-08
    politicians in (*see under* Politicians)
    public distribution system in, 168
        prices under, 168
    secularism in, 29
    textiles, 107, 119
    wars with Pakistan, 46
    women in, 82

Instrument of Accession (of Kashmir), 45, 86
Intellectuals, ii, 7, 131, 132, 137, 180
Inter-Services Intelligence (ISI), 33, 36
International Monetary Fund (IMF), 100, 111, 147, 164
    on India's growth record, 169
Intellectual property rights, 99, 104, 110, 112, 113, 114, 115, 126-27
    and obligations to India, 114-16

Japan, 98, 101, 125, 181

Kashmir, 6, 7, 23, 24-52, 88, 107, 140, 178
    as a Muslim majority state, 45
    dispute between India and Pakistan on, 24, 28, 48, 85
    elected government in, 47
        dismissal of, 47
    elections in, 30, 47, 52
    human rights in, 111
    infiltration from Pakistan in, 26
    Instrument of Accession, 45

INDEX

Kashmir.....contd
    invasion by tribesmen from Pakistan, 45
    Muslims in, 45
    plebiscite in, 30, 46, 48
    relations with Centre, 47
    terrorism in, 48, 88
        Pakistan's role in exporting, 48
Korea, North, 84
Korea, South, 84

Lending Institutions, International, 6, 13

Nehru, Jawaharlal, 191
    call for ban on nuclear tests, 191
Non-governmental organisations (NGOs), iv, 109, 173-87
    and disarmament, 182
    and environment, 184
    and human rights, 179
    and United Nations, 173
    in developing countries, 174
    role of, 173
Nuclear non-proliferation treaty (NPT), 193, 195
    India's views on, 193

Pakistan, 4, 24, 26, 28, 29, 34, 35, 41, 45, 46, 48, 50, 52, 107, 140, 174, 180, 186, 201, 208
Peres, Shimon, 84, 93
Politicians, Indian, i, ii, iii, 3, 5, 6, 8, 10, 11, 29, 33, 79, 80, 81, 85, 87, 106, 109, 153, 164, 177, 204
    complexes of, 85-86
    security of, 92-93
    working style of, 87-94, 107
Poverty, 9, 13, 14, 146, 151, 153, 163, 168
    as a political issue, 14
    Planning Commission on, 168

Reagan, Ronald, 105
Research and Analysis Wing (RAW), 33, 36
Riots, 29
Russia, 192, 200, 203, 213
    and CTBT, 200, 203
    and nuclear tests, 213

Saudi Arabia,
    and human rights, 24
Security Council, 17, 46
    permanent members of, 192
Singh, Maharaja Hari, 44, 45

INDEX 219

Sri Lanka, 4
Structural adjustment programmes (SAP), 166

Telecommunications, 55-76, 124
  competition in, 70
  private sector investment in, 65
Telecom 1995, 56, 57, 61, 62
Teresa, Mother, 106
Trade related intellectual property rights (TRIPS) (see under intellectual property rights)

Unemployment, 146
United Kingdom (UK), 192, 195, 199, 200, 209
  and CTBT, 200
  nuclear tests and, 209
United Nations, 12, 23, 25, 145, 154
Universal Declaration of Human Rights,
  objectives of, 23

Uruguay Round, negotiations, 97-99, 109, 11, 118, 167
  aims of, 97
  and developing countries, 97-102
  Indian standpoint on, 122, 167
  issues discussed in, 98-99
UN Charter, 23
UN Commission for Human Rights (UNHRC), 23, 27, 179
  achievements of, 23
  as anti-Islamic body, 24
  role of, 23-24

Women, 82, 83
World Bank, ii, 3, 4, 7, 17, 18, 86, 100, 106, 111, 147, 150, 164, 165, 166, 167, 186
World Trade Organisation (WTO), 22, 55, 56, 100, 106, 111, 114, 117, 124
World Economic Forum, 79, 80

Yeltsin, Boris, 204